TAKE THE TOUR
For a Taste of Colonial Edenton

Recipes From

St. Paul's Episcopal Church
Edenton, N.C.

FRONT COVER — THE COURTHOUSE GREEN

Edenton Bay's blue water greets the tree-lined green, graced by the Chowan County Courthouse. Built in 1767, this National Historic Landmark is said to be the finest example of Georgian architecture in the South. An excellent combination of British architecture, local artistry, and native materials, it is one of the oldest courthouses in continuous use in the country.

The Courthouse Green has been public property since 1712. During the Revolution, it was the site for drill practice. Through the years, it has hosted a variety of public events, memorials, and celebrations. Even today, it is the focus for many town events, and Edenton children are often found playing in the shade of its trees.

Copyright © 1995
St. Paul's Episcopal Church Women of Edenton, North Carolina
Printed in the United States of America
1st Printing, February 1995 — 5,000
2nd Printing, February 1999 — 5,000
ISBN: 0-9643218-0-7

This charming teapot symbol highlights helpful cooking hints relating to the recipes in *Take The Tour*. It is an artist's rendering of the bronze teapot, located east of the Courthouse Green, as pictured on the back cover. The teapot commemorates the Edenton Tea Party of 1774, when local women gathered and signed a proclamation stating they would no longer use British tea. Penelope Barker hosted this event, said to be the earliest recorded political activity by colonial women.

Printed in the USA by

WIMMER
The Wimmer Companies
Memphis
1-800-548-2537

TABLE OF CONTENTS

Proceeds from the sale of *Take The Tour* will be used to support the many outreach projects of St. Paul's Episcopal Church Women. The numerous programs range from supporting the local Food Pantry and Operation Santa Claus, to aiding Migrant Farm Workers' Ministry and Thompson's Children's Home.

ABOUT THE ARTISTS

The pen and ink sketches found throughout *Take The Tour* have been reproduced from original drawings done by the members of St. Paul's Church. The following artists have graciously donated their time and talent to illustrate this cookbook.

T. JOHN F. BECKER
DEBRA ELLIS BOYLE
CAROLYN SMITH BURNS
SUSAN DOTTERER DIXON
MISSIE CAPEHART HARRELL
HILLARY LYN KRELL
CAROL ELLISON SIECK
LOU SAYLOR SYKES

ROBIN SAMS

The cover artist, Robin Sams, discovered Edenton by sailboat after cruising for over a year in Maine and the Bahamas. She loves living on a Chowan County farm and has established Peace & Plenty Studio near Tyner. The artist has a Bachelor of Fine Arts degree from The Rhode Island School of Design. She has worked as a commercial artist in the United States and Europe and now concentrates on fine art.

Take The Tour ... For a Taste of Colonial Edenton and open the door to this charming town on Northeastern North Carolina's Albemarle Sound. The recipes invite you into the kitchens of this unique coastal village, full of history and hospitality.

As visitors walk along the sidewalks of the town, the past unfolds with each step. Established in the late sixteen hundreds, the colonial port was a bustling center of political, cultural, and commercial activity, even before the town was incorporated in 1722.

In the seventeen hundreds, as Edenton grew, so did its national prominence. Many of its citizens had significant roles in the Revolutionary years of the Colonies. Joseph Hewes, a signer of the Declaration of Independence, Hugh Williamson, who signed the United States Constitution, and James Iredell, appointed to the Supreme Court by George Washington, all resided here.

Edenton is of valuable historical significance because many of its early homes and public buildings remain. The plan of the colonial town was surveyed and drawn by the Frenchman, C.J. Sauthier, in 1769. The streets and various buildings, drawn and numbered on the Sauthier map,* are found today, beautifully restored, on contemporary Edenton's walking tour.

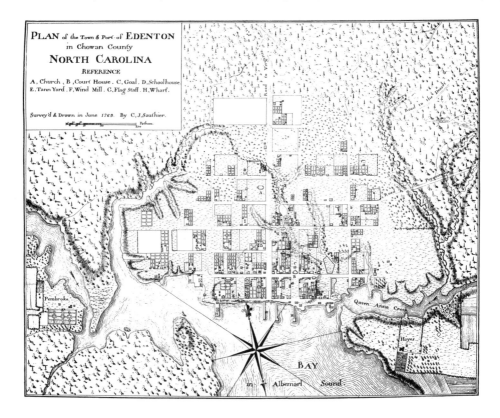

The charm of the town today is the result of an interesting twist of circumstances. The completion of the Dismal Swamp Canal and the people's opposition to a railroad connection served to isolate the area and diminish its early growth. Progress and prosperity came slowly to Edenton, sparing it the destructive side effects of rapid expansion, thus, preserving much of its Colonial architecture.

After the Civil War, a telegraph line, a steamboat line and, finally, the railroad opened trade and travel routes. The construction of the Chowan River Bridge in 1927 and the Albemarle Sound Bridge in 1938 ended the earlier isolation of the area. Along with an expanded economy came a broader awareness and appreciation of Edenton's colorful and historic heritage. Today, residents take great pride and exert enormous energy in support of historic preservation in their community.

Edenton offers a variety of opportunities to experience its history. Starting at the Visitor's Center, guided walking tours invite the tourist to explore a number of public houses and buildings, while a self guided adventure weaves through quiet tree-lined neighborhoods and wanders past busy store fronts.

Central to the town and lives of Edentonians is the elegant Chowan County Courthouse and the green that stretches to Edenton Bay. Built in 1767, the fine Georgian Courthouse remains one of the oldest in continuous use in the United States. The Courthouse Green, as depicted on the cover of *Take The Tour*, has remained public property since 1712. It is used today much as it was in colonial days for town festivals, art shows, quiet picnics and children's games.

Edenton hosts a number of special events each year. A highlight of the town's Christmas celebration is a Candlelight Tour of beautifully decorated private homes and public buildings. The Cupola House is well-known for its traditional holiday Wassail Bowl, and the Iredell House delights visitors with its re-creation of a colonial "Groaning Board". The town's residents generously open their historic homes to visitors during the Edenton Pilgrimage, held in the spring of odd numbered years. Not only are some of the town's most handsome homes open to the public, but the wonderful gardens found around every corner are in glorious bloom.

The flavorful journey, found on these pages, will inspire you to visit and discover for yourself the beauty, charm and warmth of this southern coastal village. The recipes collected are tried and true favorites of the Church Women of St. Paul's Episcopal Church. Ranging from long time family traditions to contemporary cuisine, some have been named for interesting places in the Albemarle area. Like the town itself, it is a unique blend of the excellence of the old and the vitality of the new. *Take The Tour* ... for a Taste of Colonial Edenton!

* Source: North Carolina Division of Archives and History. Original is found in the Map Room of the British Museum.

The Historic Edenton Walking Tour map is a detailed illustration of the town's streets and points of historic interest. The streets found here, and many of the buildings, are also noted on the Sauthier map. The houses, highlighted on the walking tour map and used to illustrate the cookbook sections, are listed below. The map is reproduced courtesy of Edenton Historical Commission.

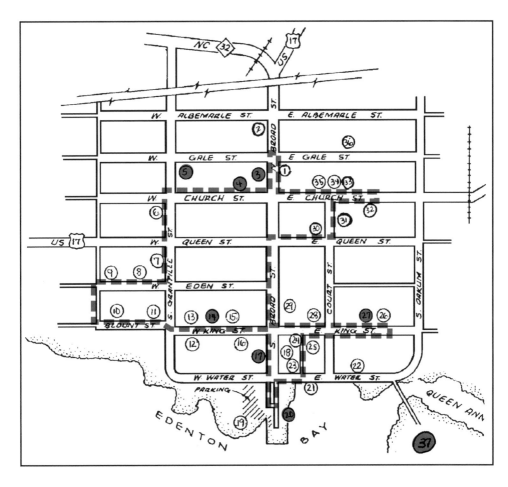

3. St. Paul's Episcopal Church - begun 1736
4. Rector's Study - circa 1850
5. Booth House - circa 1779
14. Beverly Hall - 1810
17. Cupola House - circa 1758
20. Barker-Moore House - 1782
27. Hatch-Bruer-Davis House - 1744
37. Hayes Plantation - circa 1810

ST. PAUL'S EPISCOPAL CHURCH

Spartan and dignified, St. Paul's Episcopal Church rests quietly in its serene churchyard. Organized in 1701, it was the first parish in the colony. Described as an ideal village church, St. Paul's was begun in 1736 and completed some thirty years later. The building has twice undergone extensive repairs; in 1806, William Nichols added the steeple and installed the present woodwork, and in 1949, when the galleries, roof and steeple were destroyed by fire. Because all the furnishings and the flooring had been removed for renovation, it stands today just as when Nichols finished his work.

Today, St. Paul's Episcopal Church remains an active parish.

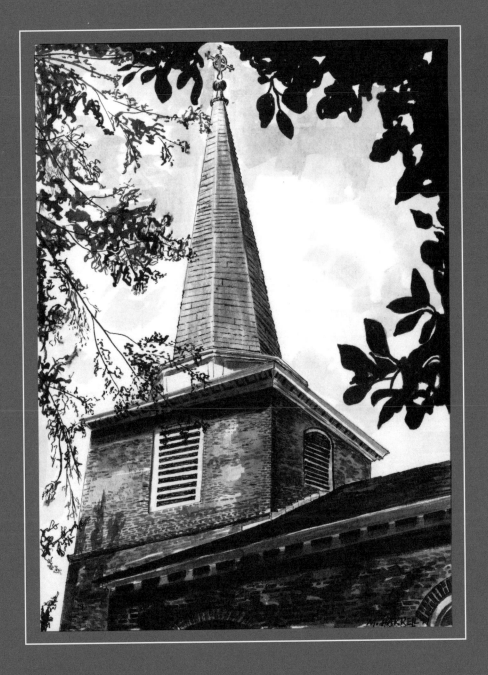

Appetizers and Beverages

APPETIZERS AND BEVERAGES

MARBELIZED MUSHROOMS

3	pounds mushrooms	1	cup vegetable oil
1	teaspoon salt	½	teaspoon white pepper
1	pinch crushed red pepper	¼	cup sugar
¼	teaspoon black pepper	1	tablespoon chopped red
½	teaspoon oregano		onion
½	teaspoon minced garlic	2	cups red wine vinegar

Put mushrooms in a large bowl; mix remaining ingredients and pour over mushrooms. Cover and marinate 3 days or more. Will keep a month under refrigeration.

Yield: Approximately 25 servings

GREEN OLIVE TAPENADE

4	dozen green olives, without pimientos	1	garlic clove, minced
		⅓	cup olive oil
2	anchovies, finely chopped or 1 squirt anchovy paste	½	lemon, juiced
		2	teaspoons cognac

Chop olives and combine with remaining ingredients. Serve on toasted pita or French bread.

Yield: 1½ cups

LEARY HOUSE MEXICAN SALSA

4	large tomatoes, diced	½	cup chopped onion
3	(4 ounce) cans black olives, sliced	2	tablespoons Italian dressing
1	(4.5 ounce) can green chilies, chopped		Salt and pepper to taste

Mix all ingredients well, chill and serve with tortilla chips.

Yield: 1 to 1½ cups

SPINACH-MUSHROOM CHEESECAKE

¾ cup Italian seasoned
breadcrumbs
¼ cup melted butter,
divided
1 (10 ounce) package frozen
chopped spinach, thawed
1 cup chopped fresh
mushrooms
¼ cup finely chopped onion
2 garlic cloves, minced
1 (2 ounce) jar diced
pimiento, drained

16 ounces softened cream
cheese
1 (7 ounce) package feta
cheese, drained
⅓ cup milk
4 large eggs
¾ teaspoon salt
¼ teaspoon ground red
pepper
¼ teaspoon ground black
pepper
⅛ teaspoon ground nutmeg

Preheat oven to 300°. Grease bottom and sides of a 9-inch springform pan. Dust sides with 1 tablespoon of breadcrumbs. Combine remaining breadcrumbs and 2 tablespoons of butter and press into bottom of pan. Set aside. Drain spinach. Sauté mushrooms, onion, and garlic in remaining 2 tablespoons butter in large skillet, stirring constantly for 3 minutes or until crisp-tender. Stir in spinach and pimiento; set aside. Beat cream cheese until creamy; blend in feta cheese. Gradually add milk, beating at low speed until blended. Add eggs, one at a time, beating after each addition. Stir in spinach mixture, salt, and remaining ingredients. Pour into pan. Bake for 1 hour until almost set. Turn oven off and partially open door; leave cheesecake in oven 1 hour. Remove and cool completely on a wire rack. Cover and chill. Serve with crackers.

Yield: 25 servings

BACON & AVOCADO DIP

3	bacon slices	2	ripe avocados
1	small tomato	1	tablespoon lemon juice
2	(4.5 ounce) cans green chili peppers	2	green onions, chopped
		¼	teaspoon salt

Cook bacon until crisp and drain on paper towels. Cool and crumble; set aside. Peel, seed and chop tomato. Seed and chop peppers. Mash avocados and stir in lemon juice, onions, salt, tomato, chili peppers and bacon. Cover and refrigerate 1 to 2 hours. Serve with tortilla chips or corn chips for dippers.

Yield: 2 cups

LAYERED CRABMEAT

16	ounces soft cream cheese	1	small garlic clove, minced
1	small onion, grated	¼	teaspoon salt
2	tablespoons Worcestershire sauce	1	cup cocktail sauce
2	tablespoons mayonnaise	1	pound backfin crabmeat
1	tablespoon lemon juice		Parsley

Mix cream cheese, onion, Worcestershire sauce, mayonnaise, lemon juice, garlic and salt with electric mixer and spread in 12-inch round dish. Spread cocktail sauce on top. Sprinkle crabmeat on top and serve with crackers.

 Crabmeat can be added to cream cheese mixture, reserving a little for the top. Delicious on cucumber slices.

Yield: 25 servings

GOOSE POND PÂTÉ

½	tablespoon unflavored gelatin	1	(9 ounce) roll Braunschweiger
½	cup water	8	ounces cream cheese
1	(10½ ounce) can beef consommé	1	teaspoon Worcestershire sauce
		1	pinch onion or garlic salt

Soften gelatin in cool water; add consommé and heat until gelatin dissolves. Blend sausage, cream cheese, Worcestershire sauce and salt. Divide the gelatin mixture into two 1½-cup molds and let set 30 minutes. Top with liver mixture and refrigerate. Unmold onto dish and serve with crackers.

 Can decorate gelatin layer with parsley leaves.

Yield: 2 molds

WATER STREET DILLY SHRIMP

2	pounds shrimp	1	large red onion, thinly sliced
⅓	cup lemon juice		
¼	cup sugar	2	tablespoons dried dill
½	cup sour cream	¼	teaspoon salt
½-1	cup mayonnaise		

Cook shrimp in boiling water until pink. Do not over cook! Cool and remove shells; combine with remaining ingredients and mix well. Cover and chill overnight.

Yield: 25 servings

STRAWBERRY HILL SHRIMP

1½	pounds shrimp	2	teaspoons salt
1	(10½ ounce) can tomato soup	½	teaspoon pepper
		10-15	bay leaves
1	cup oil	6	small white onions, thinly sliced
½	cup vinegar		
2	tablespoons sugar	3	lemons, thinly sliced
1	tablespoon Worcestershire sauce		

Cook and devein shrimp. Mix soup, oil, vinegar, sugar, Worcestershire sauce, salt and pepper and heat for 12 minutes. Layer bay leaves, onions, lemons, and shrimp in dish and cover with sauce. Marinate in refrigerator overnight. To serve, arrange shrimp on a platter and garnish with lemon and onion slices. Discard bay leaves and arrange mint or any preferred greenery around edge of platter. Provide picks or cocktail forks.

Yield: 10 to 12 servings

MARINATED SHRIMP

Shrimp

5	pounds shrimp	1	(3½ ounce) jar capers
1	purple onion		

Sauce

1	cup salad oil	2	teaspoons sugar
¾	cup vinegar	2	teaspoons salt
1	tablespoon Tabasco sauce	½	teaspoon pepper
1½	tablespoons Worcestershire sauce		Chopped parsley for garnish

Peel, clean and steam shrimp. Slice onion into rings and drain capers. Place all in a large container.

Combine sauce ingredients and pour over shrimp, onion rings and capers. Refrigerate for 24 hours, stirring occasionally. Drain well before serving. Some of the onion rings and capers may be sprinkled over the shrimp along with parsley for garnish.

Yield: 25 servings

BASIL-BLUE CHEESE TERRINE

8	ounces cream cheese	¼	cup olive oil
4	ounces blue cheese	¼	cup chopped walnuts or
1	cup spinach leaves		pecans
¾	cup fresh parsley	1	cup Parmesan cheese
¼	cup basil leaves	¼	cup slivered sun-dried
1	teaspoon minced garlic		tomatoes

Mix cheeses until smooth. Combine spinach, parsley, basil, and garlic in processor. Drizzle in oil and process until smooth. Add nuts and Parmesan cheese. Line a 5½x2½-inch loaf pan with plastic wrap and spread: one-third cheese/one-half pesto/one-half sun-dried tomatoes. Repeat. Put cheese on top. Chill 24 hours. Invert on serving platter and serve with French bread slices.

 Really special!

Yield: 1 loaf

CHEDDAR CHEESE BISCUITS

½	cup butter (no substitute)	1	cup sifted flour
½	pound grated sharp		Pinch red pepper
	Cheddar cheese		Pecan halves

Cream butter and cheese. Sift flour with red pepper and slowly add to creamed mixture. Roll into log and chill for a few hours. Slice ¼-inch thick. Place on ungreased cookie sheet. Place pecan halves in center of each biscuit. Bake in preheated 425° oven for 8 to 10 minutes.

Yield: 1 dozen

ROQUEFORT CHEESE SOUFFLÉ

1	envelope unflavored gelatin	4	ounces Roquefort cheese
2	tablespoons cool water	1	teaspoon Dijon mustard
4	tablespoons softened butter	1	egg, separated
4	ounces softened cream cheese	½	cup whipping cream, whipped

Soften gelatin in cool water and gently stir over low heat to dissolve. In food processor, blend butter and cheeses; add egg yolk, mustard and gelatin. Beat egg white until stiff, but not dry, and gently fold into gelatin mixture. Fold in cream. Prepare a 1-cup soufflé dish with a collar of oiled waxed paper or foil. Tie to dish with string. Spoon mixture into the dish so that it comes up to the top of the collar. Chill for several hours or overnight. Remove collar and serve with crackers or raw vegetables.

Yield: 4 to 6 servings

SKINNER-BOND HOUSE CHEESE DUNK

2	cups drained cottage cheese	1	tablespoon prepared mustard
1	cup grated sharp Cheddar cheese	3	green onions, finely chopped
2	ounces crumbled Roquefort or blue cheese	¼	teaspoon salt
3	tablespoons mayonnaise	⅛	teaspoon pepper
2	tablespoons prepared horseradish	2	apples, sliced
		2	pears, sliced

In a medium bowl, blend together cottage cheese, Cheddar cheese, Roquefort cheese, mayonnaise, horseradish, mustard, onions, salt and pepper. Spoon into a medium serving bowl. Serve with apples, pears and potato chips for dipping.

Yield: 3 cups

CRANBERRY-AMARETTO CHUTNEY WITH CREAM CHEESE

8	ounces softened cream cheese	½	teaspoon lemon rind
2	cups fresh cranberries	¼	cup Amaretto
1	cup sugar	1	tablespoon orange marmalade
1	tablespoon plus 1 teaspoon lemon juice		

Line a 2-cup mold with damp cheesecloth, letting cloth hang over edges. Firmly press cream cheese, one spoonful at a time, into prepared mold. Fold cheesecloth over top; cover and chill for 6 hours. Combine cranberries, sugar, and lemon juice in small saucepan. Cook over medium heat, stirring constantly, until mixture comes to a boil; reduce heat and simmer 20 minutes. Remove from heat; add lemon rind, Amaretto, and marmalade, stirring until blended. Cool mixture to room temperature. Unmold cheese onto serving plate. Remove cheesecloth; spoon cranberry sauce over cheese. Serve with crackers.

 Sauce may be served hot or cold with meat.

Yield: 20 servings

CREAM CHEESE AND SUN-DRIED TOMATOES

½	(8 ounce) jar sun-dried tomatoes packed in oil	Basil or parsley leaf to taste
8	ounces cream cheese	

Drain and quarter tomatoes. Spread crackers or thinly sliced French bread with cream cheese. Garnish with basil or parsley leaf and a piece of tomato.

 If unable to find tomatoes in oil, use recipe for Sun-dried Tomatoes in Vermicelli.

Yield: 8 to 10 servings

JEZEBEL JELLY

1	(8 ounce) jar pineapple preserves	1	(5 ounce) jar prepared horseradish
1	(8 ounce) jar apple jelly	1	tablespoon cracked pepper
1-2	tablespoons dry mustard	8	ounces cream cheese

Mix preserves, jelly, mustard, horseradish and pepper together until smooth and spread over cream cheese. Serve with crackers.

 A wonderful "last minute" hors d'oeuvre!

Yield: 2 cups

CURRY DIP

16	ounces cream cheese	½	cup chopped pecans
1	cup slightly chopped chutney	½	teaspoon dry mustard
		2	teaspoons curry powder

Mix all ingredients together and chill for 2 hours. Serve with your favorite crackers.

 Simple and fantastic!

Yield: 3 cups

EGG-CAVIAR "CAKE"

12	hard-boiled eggs, finely chopped	8	ounces softened cream cheese
6	tablespoons mayonnaise	1	cup sour cream
2	large white onions, chopped	1	(5 ounce) jar red caviar Lemon and parsley

Mix eggs and mayonnaise. Spread on bottom of springform pan. Top with onion. Whip cream cheese with sour cream and ice "cake" with mixture. Spread caviar on top. Refrigerate overnight. Garnish with lemon wedges and parsley. Serve with melba toast.

Yield: 50 servings

ROQUEFORT CHEESE TORTE

½	cup Parmesan cheese	4	eggs
½	cup dried breadcrumbs	1	tablespoon Tabasco sauce
¾	pound bacon	2½	tablespoons
1	small yellow onion		Worcestershire sauce
16	ounces cream cheese		Parsley
8	ounces Roquefort cheese		

Preheat oven to 350°. Butter and coat bottom of 9 or 10-inch springform pan with Parmesan cheese and breadcrumbs. Set aside. Cook bacon until crisp; drain. Finely chop bacon and onion in food processor. Blend cheeses in mixing bowl until smooth. Add remaining ingredients and bacon/onion mixture. Pour into prepared pan; bake 1 hour. Turn oven off and let sit 1 hour. Chill overnight. Unmold, garnish with parsley and serve with French bread slices or crackers.

Yield: 40 servings

PROVINCIAL STUFFED EGGS

10	hard-boiled eggs	2	teaspoons white wine
½	cup Mediterranean olives		vinegar
	(black, wrinkled kind)	¼	cup extra-virgin olive oil
1	ounce flat anchovy fillets	¼	teaspoon freshly ground
1	tablespoon capers		pepper
1	large garlic clove, crushed	2	dashes cayenne pepper
	and pressed		Tiny capers for garnish

Halve eggs and remove yolks. Set aside one half of a yolk for garnish. Rinse and pit olives; rinse and pat dry anchovy fillets. Combine olives, anchovies, capers and garlic; process in blender until chopped. Add the egg yolks, olive oil, black pepper and cayenne. Process this mixture to coarse paste. Spoon into egg-white halves, mounding in center. Sieve the reserved egg-yolk half; garnish each egg with a pinch of sieved yolk and a tiny caper.

Yield: 20 egg halves

HOT AND COLD CHEESE APPETIZER

¼	cup finely chopped fresh parsley	2	cups shredded Muenster cheese
¼	cup finely chopped fresh chives	⅛	cup Dijon mustard
6	ounces softened cream cheese	2	garlic cloves, crushed
		1	medium onion, finely minced
2	cups shredded sharp Cheddar cheese	⅛	teaspoon Tabasco sauce

Mix the parsley and chives; set aside. In large bowl, mix remaining ingredients and divide mixture in half. Place one half in a serving dish and sprinkle with half the parsley and chives. Cover and refrigerate. Preheat oven to 375°. Place remaining mixture in small ovenproof baking dish and stir in remaining parsley and chives. Bake for 15 minutes. Serve with apple slices and crackers.

 This recipe, served both hot and cold, gives a completely different taste. May be made ahead, cooking hot portion just before serving.

Yield: 30 servings

CHEDDAR PUFFS

½	cup softened butter	1¼	cups sifted flour
1	cup grated sharp Cheddar cheese	½	teaspoon salt

Preheat oven to 400°. Cream together butter and cheese until smooth. Blend in flour and salt; knead lightly. Using a teaspoon, shape into small balls. Place on greased baking sheet. Bake for 12 minutes or until golden.

 Freezes well. Cook while frozen.

Yield: 3 dozen puffs

SUPER BOWL DIP

1	loaf oval-shaped rye bread	8	ounces grated sharp Cheddar cheese
3	tablespoons butter	⅓	cup grated Parmesan cheese
3	tablespoons flour		Pepper to taste
1¼	cups beer		Pimiento strips

Preheat oven to 350°. Cut a thin oval slice from top of bread using a serrated knife. Remove center; cut bread into cubes. Place on cookie sheet and toast. Melt butter over medium heat and stir in flour. Remove from heat and gradually add beer. Return to heat; bring to a boil and add Cheddar, Parmesan, and pepper. Stir until melted and pour into bread. Replace bread top. Bake for 20 to 25 minutes. Remove from oven and arrange pimiento on top to resemble football. Dip toasted bread cubes in hot cheese.

Yield: 12 servings

MYSTIC CHILI DIP

8	ounces cream cheese	8	ounces Monterey Jack jalapeño cheese
1	can chili without beans	3	scallions, chopped

Preheat oven to 350°. Combine cheeses and chili and mix well. Put in flat casserole and top with scallions. Bake for 25 minutes or until cheese melts and bubbles. Serve with tortilla chips.

 Men love this!

Yield: 6 to 8 servings

ARTICHOKE PIE

4-5	garlic cloves, crushed	¼	cup grated Parmesan cheese
1	medium onion, thinly sliced		Salt and pepper to taste
1	tablespoon butter	1	(14 ounce) can artichoke hearts
3	large eggs		
1	cup whipping cream	1	unbaked 9-inch pastry shell
½	cup shredded mozzarella cheese		

Preheat oven to 400°. Sauté garlic and onion in butter until golden; do not brown. Beat eggs and add cream, cheeses, salt, pepper and garlic/onion mixture. Drain artichokes and cut into quarters. Add to egg mixture and gently pour into pastry shell. Bake for about 45 minutes until set. Cut into wedges and serve warm or cold.

 This may be served as an entree with a green salad.

Yield: 16 servings

BLACK-EYED DIP

2	cups refried beans	1	(4 ounce) can chopped green chili peppers, drained
½	envelope chili or taco seasoning mix		
1	cup sour cream	1	ripe tomato, chopped
3	green onions, chopped	¼	cup chopped black olives
		8	ounces Monterey Jack cheese, shredded

Mix refried beans with seasoning mix. Spread in bottom of shallow casserole. Cover with sour cream, sealing edges. Add remaining ingredients. Sprinkle shredded cheese over the top. Put under broiler until cheese melts. Serve with tortilla chips.

 May be microwaved for 3 minutes to melt cheese.

Yield: 6 to 8 servings

KITCHEN GARDEN SPREAD

⅓	cup olive oil	1	(6 ounce) can tomato paste
3	cups peeled and cubed eggplant	¾	cup chopped ripe olives
⅓	cup chopped green pepper	½	teaspoon oregano
		½	teaspoon pepper
1	onion, chopped	2	tablespoons wine vinegar
1	(4 ounce) can sliced mushrooms	1½	teaspoons sugar
		1	teaspoon salt
2	garlic cloves, crushed		Tabasco sauce to taste

Heat oil and add eggplant, green pepper, onion, mushrooms, and garlic. Cover and cook for 10 minutes; stir. Add remaining ingredients and simmer for 30 to 40 minutes. Serve hot with corn chips or crackers.

 May be prepared ahead. This freezes well before cooking.

Yield: 6 to 8 servings

HEARTHSTONE BACON AND MUSHROOMS

6	bacon slices	1	envelope Lipton golden onion soup
½	pound mushrooms, sliced thin	8	ounces cream cheese
2	garlic cloves, minced	8	ounces sour cream
			Pepper

Microwave bacon in 2-quart casserole until crisp. Add garlic and mushrooms to drippings and bacon; cook for 3 minutes. Chop bacon in dish and add soup and cream cheese. Microwave until cheese is melted; add sour cream and cook until hot. Serve with crackers.

Yield: 8 to 10 servings

M^CMULLAN HOUSE MUSHROOM PUFFS

Pastry

3	ounces softened cream cheese	½	cup softened butter
		1½	cups flour

Filling

1	small onion, minced	½	teaspoon salt
3	tablespoons butter	2	tablespoons flour
½	pound mushrooms, minced	¼	cup sour cream
			Pepper to taste
¼	teaspoon thyme		

Preheat oven to 450°. Mix cream cheese and butter. Stir in flour and blend well. Chill 30 minutes before rolling. In skillet, sauté onion in butter. Add mushrooms and cook 3 minutes. Add thyme, salt and pepper; blend well. Sprinkle flour over mixture. Add sour cream and cook until thickened. Do not boil. Remove from heat and chill. On a floured board, roll out dough until very thin. Cut 3-inch rounds and place a bit less than 1 teaspoon of filling on each. Fold edges over and press together with fork tines. Prick with fork. Bake for 15 minutes on ungreased cookie sheet.

 These freeze well. Do not thaw before baking.

Yield: 40-50 puffs

GARLIC POTATOES

25	tiny new potatoes, scrubbed		Salt and pepper to taste
½	cup butter	½	cup chopped fresh parsley
½	cup olive oil	1	tablespoon dill weed
		2	garlic cloves, minced

Boil potatoes until just tender, about 10 minutes. Drain. In a medium skillet, heat the butter and oil over medium-low heat. Add garlic and sauté for 3 to 5 minutes. Remove from heat. Add sauce to warm potatoes and mix gently. Add parsley and dill weed to lightly cover. Let marinate in refrigerator for 2 days. Serve at room temperature with toothpicks.

   Can also be served hot.

Yield: 25 servings

MULLEN HOUSE POTATO SKINS

5	large russet potatoes	¾	cup grated Monterey Jack cheese
⅓	cup melted butter		
¾	cup grated Cheddar cheese		

Bake potatoes at 450° for 1 hour. When cool enough to handle, cut each lengthwise into quarters. Scoop out insides, leaving a ⅛ inch shell. Brush skins inside and out with butter. Place, cut side up, on baking sheet and bake at 500° for about 12 minutes or until crisp. Remove from oven and distribute cheese evenly. Broil 4 inches from heat until cheeses melt, about 2 minutes. Serve hot.

   Use potato insides to make a favorite potato casserole.

Yield: 20 servings

CHERRY POINT SPINACH SQUARES

1	pound Muenster cheese, sliced	4	ounces feta cheese
3	(8 ounce) packages frozen chopped spinach	2	eggs, beaten
		¼	teaspoon pepper
1	large onion	1½	teaspoons dill weed
1	cup fat free cottage cheese	2	large garlic cloves, minced

Preheat oven to 350°. Line bottom of a 9x13-inch glass dish with cheese slices. Cook spinach in microwave as directed. Press out all liquid. Chop onion; microwave for 1 minute. Combine all ingredients in large bowl; mix well. Spread over cheese and bake for 45 minutes. Cool slightly before cutting into squares.

 This makes a delicious quiche. Line an unbaked deep dish pie shell with cheese and follow above directions.

Yield: 25 servings

BAYVIEW CHICKEN WINGS

1	cup soy sauce	1	cup brown sugar
1	cup white wine	50	chicken wings

Preheat oven to 400°. Mix soy sauce, wine and sugar until well blended. Lay wings flat in a single layer in large pan; cover with marinade. Bake for 1 hour, until brown and crisp.

 It is not necessary to turn wings during cooking.

Yield: 25 servings

JAIL HOUSE DOGS

2	pounds hot dogs	½	cup light brown sugar
½	can beer	1	(16 ounce) bottle ketchup
1	cup light Karo syrup		

Combine all ingredients except hot dogs and bring to a boil. Cut hot dogs into bite-size pieces and add to mixture; simmer 30 minutes. Serve in a chafing dish with party picks.

This is great to place near the bar because men love it! Freezes well.

Yield: 25 servings

CHEAPSIDE DIP

1	cup sour cream	1	teaspoon minced onion
1	(2¼ ounce) jar dried beef	1	teaspoon garlic salt
4	tablespoons milk	1	cup chopped pecans or
16	ounces softened cream cheese		almonds

Preheat oven to 350°. Chop beef and mix together with all ingredients except nuts; spread in ovenproof dish. Top with nuts, dot with butter and bake for 20 minutes. Serve with crackers.

Yield: 2½ cups

TANGY MEATBALL APPETIZERS

2	pounds bulk pork sausage	1	(8 ounce) bottle chutney
1	cup sour cream	½	cup sherry

Preheat oven to 350°. Form sausage into balls and place on cookie sheet. Bake for 30 minutes until brown; pour off grease. Mix sour cream, chutney and sherry. Combine with meat balls and simmer until warm. (Do not boil as the sour cream will curdle.) Put into a warmed chafing dish and provide toothpicks for serving.

 The meatballs can be done ahead and frozen.

Yield: 100 meatballs

CASON HOUSE CRAB MORNAY

1	cup butter	1	pound grated Swiss cheese
2	bunches green onions, chopped	2	pounds crabmeat
½	cup chopped parsley		Salt and pepper to taste
4	tablespoons flour	4	tablespoons dry sherry
4	cups half-and-half cream	60-70	toast rounds or crackers

In Dutch oven, melt butter and sauté onions and parsley. Add flour; mix until smooth and stir in cream. Add cheese and allow to melt. Add crabmeat, salt and pepper. Heat thoroughly but do not boil. Stir in sherry just before serving. Serve in chaffing dish with toast rounds or crackers.

 Serves 6 to 8 as a main dish with toast points.

Yield: 25 to 30 servings

CRAB AND ARTICHOKE DIP

8	ounces shredded sharp Cheddar cheese	3	tablespoons lemon juice Freshly ground pepper
2	cups mayonnaise	1	(14 ounce) can artichoke
1	tablespoon Dijon mustard		hearts
2	teaspoons Worcestershire sauce	½	cup chopped parsley
		1	pound backfin crabmeat

Preheat oven to 250°. Combine cheese, mayonnaise, mustard, Worcestershire sauce, lemon juice and pepper; stir until well blended. Drain and chop artichoke hearts. Gently fold into mixture along with the crabmeat and parsley. Put into a 6-cup casserole and bake for 20 minutes. Serve with crackers or French bread.

Yield: 3 cups

DRUMMOND'S POINT CRABMEAT

8	ounces sharp Cheddar cheese	½	cup milk
		½	cup white wine
8	ounces Velveeta cheese	1	pound crabmeat

Cook cheeses and milk in double boiler or microwave until cheese is melted. Remove from heat; add crabmeat and wine and mix thoroughly. Serve with crackers or bite-size pastry shells.

Yield: 2 cups

CRAB MELT-A-WAYS

1	jar Olde English cheese	1	(6½ ounce) can Harris
½	cup butter		crabmeat, drained
½	teaspoon seasoning salt	12-14	thin bread slices or 1
½	teaspoon garlic salt		package English muffins
1	tablespoon mayonnaise		Paprika

Preheat oven to 375°. Blend cheese and butter together. Add seasoning salt, garlic salt, mayonnaise and crabmeat. Cut bread into quarters and spread with crabmeat mixture. Sprinkle with paprika and bake for 15 minutes.

 These may be frozen before baking. Do not thaw before cooking.

Yield: about 50

CRABMEAT HORS D'OEUVRE

½	cup butter		Salt and onion salt to taste
¼	cup flour	1	pound backfin crabmeat
2	cups half-and-half cream	⅓	cup dry sherry
	Dash of Tabasco sauce		

Melt butter in double boiler; add flour and stir until smooth. Gradually add cream and cook, stirring constantly, until thickened. Add Tabasco, salt and onion salt. Remove all shells from crabmeat. Add crabmeat and sherry to cream mixture. Heat, stirring often. Pour hot crab mixture into chafing dish. Serve with small pastry shells or melba toast rounds.

 May be made a day ahead and reheated in double boiler.

Yield: 3 cups

GATE HOUSE CRAB

1	pound crabmeat	1	cup Durkee's dressing
1	pound cooked shrimp		Salt to taste
2½	cups finely chopped celery		Red and black pepper to taste
1	large green pepper, diced	¼	teaspoon Tabasco sauce
2	medium onions, finely chopped	¼	teaspoon Worcestershire sauce
1	cup mayonnaise		

Combine crabmeat, shrimp, celery, green pepper and onions; set aside. Mix mayonnaise, Durkee's dressing, salt, peppers, Tabasco and Worcestershire sauces; add to crab/shrimp mixture. Refrigerate until ready to serve. Remove from refrigerator 1 hour before serving. Preheat oven to 350° and bake for 20 to 30 minutes. Serve on toast or crackers.

 May be mixed a day ahead and refrigerated.

Yield: 15 to 20 servings

HOT CRAB CANAPÉ PIE

1	pound lump crabmeat		Dash of Tabasco sauce
1	tablespoon horseradish	2	cups Hellmann's mayonnaise
2	tablespoons capers		
1	teaspoon grated lemon rind	¾	cup grated extra sharp Cheddar cheese
½	teaspoon Accent		

Preheat oven to 350°. Mix all ingredients together except cheese. Add more seasonings such as onion, Worcestershire sauce, herbs, etc. as desired. Spread into a 10-inch pie plate and cover the top with cheese. Bake for 20 to 25 minutes or until mixture bubbles. Encircle with crackers and serve.

 Serve over an avocado for a luncheon dish.

Yield: 25 servings

FANTASTIC SHRIMP WHEELS

1	(4½ ounce) can shrimp, drained and mashed	2	tablespoons chili sauce
¼	cup mayonnaise	1	tablespoon finely chopped celery
2	tablespoons chopped green olives	2	packages refrigerated crescent rolls

Preheat oven to 325°. Combine all ingredients, except rolls. Unroll crescent roll dough and separate crescents into 8 rectangles. Spread ¼ cup mixture on each rectangle and roll up jellyroll fashion. Cut into 7 slices each. Place on greased cookie sheet and bake for 10-12 minutes.

Yield: 56 servings

LEMON-OREGANO TUNA MOUSSE

1	(6½ ounce) can tuna packed in oil, undrained	2	tablespoons extra-virgin olive oil
4	tablespoons softened, unsalted butter	½	teaspoon dried leaf oregano
	Zest of 1 lemon	1	garlic clove, minced
2	tablespoons lemon juice		

Flake tuna with oil and place in food processor. Add remaining ingredients and process until smooth and creamy. Taste for seasoning and serve at room temperature with crackers.

 Can be stored, covered, in refrigerator for 3 days.

Yield: 1 cup

BLACKBEARD'S BOURBON SLUSH

2	tea bags	1	(6 ounce) can orange juice
1	cup boiling water	½	cup bourbon
1	cup sugar	½	cup frozen lemonade
3½	cups water		

Steep tea bags in boiling water 2 to 3 minutes. Remove bags; add sugar and remaining ingredients. Freeze. Remove 10 minutes before serving. Garnish with mint leaves.

Yield: 1½ quarts

BROAD STREET BLOODIES

1	(46 ounce) can V-8 juice	½	teaspoon Tabasco sauce
½	cup ketchup	½	teaspoon celery salt
1	teaspoon prepared horseradish	3	tablespoons lemon juice
			Dash of salt and pepper
2	tablespoons Worcestershire sauce	12	ounces vodka

Blend ingredients and pour over ice cubes. Stick a stalk of celery in the glass for garnish.

 Can be prepared ahead. Will keep in refrigerator for 2 weeks.

Yield: 6 10-ounce drinks

DUKE OF ALBEMARLE PUNCH

12	lemons, juiced	1	fifth bourbon
1	cup sugar	4	cups water
2	lemon rinds, grated		

Mix lemon juice, sugar, lemon rinds and water together and refrigerate overnight. Add bourbon and pour into punch bowl full of cracked ice.

Yield: ½ gallon

FISH HOUSE PUNCH

1½	pounds sugar	1	half gallon cognac
1	half gallon lemon juice	1	cup peach brandy
2	half gallons Jamaican rum		

Dissolve sugar in a little cold water; stir in strained lemon juice. Pour this mixture over a large solid lump of ice and add rum, cognac and peach brandy. Let mellow several hours, stirring occasionally.

Yield: 2 gallons

GOLDEN MARGARITAS

1	ounce Cuervo Gold tequila	½	ounce Rose's lime juice
½	ounce Grand Marnier	1	quart sour mix

Mix all ingredients and shake. Serve in salt-rimmed glasses and garnish with lime slices.

Yield: 1 quart

CHRISTMAS EGGNOG

8	eggs	1	cup sugar
1	quart whipping cream		Nutmeg
1	pint brandy		

Separate eggs and beat whites until stiff. Beat cream until stiff and fold in egg whites. Beat egg yolks and sugar until lemon colored; add brandy very slowly as it cooks the eggs. Keep beating until all brandy is mixed in. Fold egg white mixture into brandy mixture. If too thick, add milk. Add a shake of nutmeg to each cup when you serve.

Yield: 2 quarts

JOHN'S ISLAND RUM PUNCH

¾	pound sugar	1	quart Jamaican rum
7	cups water	1	quart light Bacardi rum
3	cups lemon juice	½	cup peach brandy

Dissolve the sugar in 3 cups of the water. Add lemon juice and rest of the water and stir. Add last 3 ingredients and let stand for 3 hours, stirring occasionally. Pour over block of ice in punch bowl.

 A fifth of St. Croix rum may be added to stretch this recipe.

Yield: 25 servings

SHERRY SOURS

1	bottle pale dry sherry	Ice cubes
2	(6 ounce) cans frozen lemonade	

Combine undiluted lemonade with equal parts of sherry. Put in blender with ice cubes and frappé.

Yield: 4 servings

VELVET HAMMER

1	quart vanilla ice cream	Bourbon to taste
2	tablespoons Kahlua	(optional)
2	tablespoons dark rum	

Place all ingredients in a blender and mix well. Make ahead and freeze in plastic containers. Blend again when ready to serve.

 Serve in crystal stemware.

Yield: 8 servings

WISTERIA TEA PUNCH

1	(6-ounce) can concentrated apple juice	2	cups apricot nectar
		½	gallon orange sherbet
1	(6-ounce) can concentrated orange juice	3	quarts 7-up
		1-2	cups bourbon

Mix first 3 ingredients. Cube sherbet and add to mixture. Add 7-up and bourbon and serve.

Yield: Enough for a crowd!

CUPOLA HOUSE WASSAIL

1	gallon apple cider	4	sticks cinnamon
2	(12 ounce) cans frozen lemonade	5	dried apple rings
		½	orange, thinly sliced
1	tablespoon ground cloves	½	lemon, thinly sliced
½	teaspoon ground allspice	1	quart white wine

Mix first 5 ingredients in large enamel or stainless steel pot. Heat to boiling and simmer 10 to 15 minutes. Place fruit in bottom of punch bowl. Add wine. Pour cider mixture over fruit and wine. Serve.

 To double or triple the recipe, decrease the spices somewhat.

Yield: 25 servings

EDMUND HATCH HOUSE

A stroll under the crepe myrtles of East King Street brings into view the elaborate chimney of the Edmund Hatch House. The variety of brick bonds shows the numerous changes the house has undergone through many years. The western front section of the house is thought to be the oldest dwelling in Edenton, dating back to 1744. In its illustrious past, it housed O'Malley's Ordinary, a local tavern.

Carolyn Burns '94

Breads

BREADS

AUSTRIAN PANCAKE

1	cup plain, all-purpose flour	2	cups milk
2	tablespoons sugar	1	cup half-and-half cream
¾	teaspoon salt	2	tablespoons butter
3	eggs		Confectioner's sugar
			Apricot preserves

Preheat oven to 375°. Sift flour with sugar and salt; set aside. Beat eggs in a medium bowl; beat in milk and cream. Add flour mixture. Heat butter in 10-inch skillet until sizzling. Turn batter into skillet and bake for 30 minutes or until set and golden. Cut into pie slices and sprinkle with confectioner's sugar. Serve with apricot preserves.

Substitute ½ cup sifted flour and ½ cup ground pecans for the flour, and/or substitute 1 cup milk and 2 cups sour cream for the milk and cream. A few thinly sliced apples may be added to the batter. Proceed as instructed.

Yield: 6 servings

SWEDISH OVEN PANCAKE

4	bacon slices	1	cup flour
3	eggs	1	tablespoon sugar
2	cups milk	¾	teaspoon salt

Preheat oven to 375°. Cook bacon in a 9-inch skillet and pour off part of the drippings. Blend eggs, milk, flour, sugar and salt in blender. Pour mixture over bacon and bake in skillet for 30 to 35 minutes until golden.

It puffs up like Yorkshire pudding and makes a nice breakfast served with melted butter.

Serve with fresh fruit and whipped cream as a dessert.

Yield: 4 servings

BANANA PANCAKES

1	cup mashed bananas	¼	teaspoon cinnamon
3	tablespoons lemon juice	1	egg yolk, beaten
½	cup flour	¼	cup milk
1	teaspoon baking powder	1	egg white, stiffly beaten
5	tablespoons sugar		

Add lemon to mashed bananas and blend well. Add dry ingredients, egg yolk and milk. Blend well. Fold in egg white and mix well. Cook as any pancake.

 Serve with heated syrup or sprinkle with powdered sugar.

OVEN FRENCH TOAST

Bread

12	French bread slices, 1½ inches thick	½	teaspoon cinnamon
		6	eggs, beaten
8	ounces cream cheese	1	cup half-and-half cream
2	tablespoons sugar	½	cup milk
½	teaspoon nutmeg		

Strawberry Topping

1	cup powdered sugar	⅓	cup Grand Marnier
2	tablespoons cornstarch	3	cups sliced strawberries
½	cup melted butter		

Preheat oven to 350°. Slice each piece of bread horizontally to form a pocket and spread 1½ tablespoons of mixture of cream cheese, sugar, nutmeg and cinnamon inside. Place bread in greased casserole. Mix together eggs, cream and milk; pour over bread slices, turning to coat and saturate. Bake for 35 minutes.

Cook sugar, cornstarch, butter and Grand Marnier over medium heat, stirring constantly. Add strawberries and heat through. Serve on top of French toast.

 This dish can be made the night before, without topping, and refrigerated.

Yield: 12 servings

ALMOND BREAKFAST BREAD

Cake
1	cup butter, divided	3	eggs
2	cups flour, divided	1	teaspoon almond extract
1	cup plus 1 tablespoon water		

Frosting
½	cup confectioner's sugar	2	teaspoons vanilla
1	tablespoon milk	1	teaspoon almond extract
1	tablespoon melted butter	¼	cup chopped almonds

Preheat oven to 375°. Cut ½ cup butter into 1 cup flour. Add 1 table-spoon water. Blend well and divide into 2 balls. Flatten each ball into a 15x3-inch strip on a baking sheet. Bring 1 cup water and ½ cup butter to a rolling boil. Beat in 1 cup flour until smooth. Remove from heat. Beat in eggs, one at a time, and add almond extract. Spread half the mixture on each pastry strip. Bake for 40 minutes.

Blend sugar, milk, butter, vanilla and almond extract until smooth. Stir in almonds and spread on warm cakes.

Yield: 2 coffee cakes

BLUEBERRY COFFEE CAKE

Cake
2	cups Bisquick	1	cup sour cream
¼	cup sugar	1	cup blueberry pie filling
1	egg		

Topping
¼	cup sugar	1	teaspoon butter
½	teaspoon cinnamon		

Preheat oven to 400°. Combine Bisquick, sugar, egg and sour cream and beat 1 minute. Spread half the mixture in a greased 8-inch pan. Add a layer of blueberry filling. Add remaining mixture.

Mix topping and sprinkle on cake. Bake for 30 minutes.

Yield: 8 servings

SUNDAY BREAKFAST PUFF

½   cup butter   ½   cup milk
2   eggs   ½   cup flour

Preheat oven to 425°. Melt butter in iron skillet. Mix remaining ingredients until smooth. Pour mixture into hot skillet and bake for 15 minutes. Cut into wedges. Sprinkle with powdered sugar and squeeze lemon juice on top or use your favorite syrup.

 Fun and easy for children to make.

Yield: 2 servings

CHEESE DANISH

1   egg, separated   1   package crescent roll
¼   cup sugar   dough
8   ounces cream cheese   ½   cup chopped nuts
1   teaspoon vanilla

Combine egg yolk, sugar, cream cheese and vanilla. Beat until fluffy. Unroll crescent dough and pinch seams. Place on cookie sheet and spread cream cheese mixture on top, not too near edges. Bring sides and ends of rectangle in and pinch together. Brush top with egg white wash and top with nuts.

 Simple to make and very good.

CHEESY BREAKFAST RING

½	cup butter	1	cup coarsely grated
¼	teaspoon salt		Gruyère cheese
1	cup water	2	rounded teaspoons
1	cup all-purpose flour		Parmesan cheese
4	eggs		

Preheat oven to 425°. Bring butter, salt and water to a boil. When butter is totally melted, sprinkle flour into mixture stirring vigorously and constantly with a wooden spoon. Remove from heat and cool slightly. Add eggs, one at a time, beating well after each addition until dough is smooth. Add all but 3 tablespoons of the cheeses, beating constantly. When thoroughly mixed, drop dough by tablespoonfuls onto a lightly greased cookie sheet to form a completed ring. Sprinkle remaining 3 tablespoons of cheese around circular top. Bake for 10 minutes until bread is a rich golden brown. Serve hot.

Nice for brunch. Fill center of ring with scrambled eggs and bacon.

Yield: 6 servings

JUBILEE BLUES

2	cups flour	2	eggs, beaten
½	teaspoon salt	½	cup melted butter
2	teaspoons baking powder	1	cup blueberries
1¼	cups sugar		Sugar and cinnamon
½	cup milk		

Preheat oven to 350°. Sift and mix flour, salt and baking powder. Mix sugar, milk, eggs and butter; add to flour mixture. Fold in blueberries. Fill greased muffin tins two-thirds full and sprinkle with mixture of sugar and cinnamon. Bake for 30 minutes.

Chowan County raises beautiful big blueberries. Can be frozen (unwashed) and used as needed throughout the winter.

Yield: 1 dozen muffins

CARROT BLENDER MUFFINS

2	cups all-purpose flour	1	egg
2½	teaspoons baking powder	½	teaspoon vanilla
½	teaspoon salt	½	cup softened butter
2	tablespoons sugar	1	large carrot, grated
1	cup milk		

Preheat oven to 400°. Mix the first 4 ingredients together in bowl; set aside. Put remaining ingredients, except carrot, in blender and blend on low speed until well blended. Add carrot and process until thoroughly mixed. Pour over dry ingredients. Stir until just moistened. Fill 12 greased muffin tins two-thirds full. Bake for 20 to 30 minutes.

Yield: 1 dozen

WHITE-BOND HOUSE APPLE MUFFINS

1½	cups brown sugar, packed	1	teaspoon baking soda
⅔	cup vegetable oil	1	teaspoon vanilla
1	egg	2	cups flour
1	cup buttermilk	1½	cups chopped, tart apples
1	teaspoon salt	½	cup chopped nuts

Preheat oven to 350°. Mix together sugar, oil and egg until well blended. In separate bowl, mix buttermilk, salt, baking soda, and vanilla; add to egg mixture. Add flour all at once and mix until there are no dry spots. Fold in apples and nuts and fill greased muffin tins three-fourths full and bake for 30 minutes.

 The Lords Proprietors' Inn, a local B & B, serves these wonderful muffins for breakfast.

Yield: 1 dozen muffins

DATE AND NUT BRAN MUFFINS

½	cup unsalted butter	¼	teaspoon salt
1½	cups chopped pitted dates	¼	cup brown sugar
½	teaspoon vanilla		(optional)
1	egg, beaten	1	cup milk
1	cup oat bran	¾	cup chopped pecans
¾	cup cake flour	¼	cup rolled oats
4	teaspoons baking powder		

Preheat oven to 400°. Line 12 muffin tins with paper liners. Beat butter with dates until butter is light; beat in vanilla; add egg and blend well. In another bowl, combine oat bran, flour, baking powder, salt and brown sugar; mix until blended. Mix in half the milk. Add remaining flour and milk and fold in with a rubber spatula until batter just comes together. It will be lumpy. Fold in pecans. Spoon batter into tins, two-thirds full. Sprinkle each muffin with oats and bake for 30 minutes until golden brown. Let cool 5 minutes before removing from pan.

Yield: 1 dozen

PACK HOUSE PINEAPPLE MUFFINS

Muffin

4	ounces cream cheese	1	teaspoon baking soda
1	cup sugar	1	(8 ounce) can crushed
½	cup sour cream		pineapple, drained
1	egg		(reserve ½ tablespoon of
2	teaspoons vanilla		juice)
2	cups flour	¼	cup sliced almonds
1	teaspoon salt	2¼	ounces coconut flakes

Glaze

½	tablespoon melted butter	½	tablespoon pineapple
½	cup powdered sugar		juice

Preheat oven to 350°. Process cheese, sugar, sour cream, egg and vanilla in food processor until smooth. Gently mix flour, salt and baking soda. Add liquid ingredients to dry ingredients and blend well. Fold in pineapple, almonds and coconut. Grease muffin tins and fill two-thirds full and bake for 35 minutes.

Mix together butter, sugar and pineapple juice and spread on baked muffins.

Yield: 1 dozen muffins

BANANA NUT BREAD

1	cup sugar	4	tablespoons buttermilk
½	cup butter	2	cups flour
3	ripe bananas	¼	teaspoon salt
2	eggs, beaten	½	cup nuts
1	teaspoon baking soda		

Preheat oven to 350°. Dissolve baking soda in buttermilk. Cream sugar and butter. Add mashed bananas, eggs, buttermilk mixture and sifted dry ingredients. Add nuts. Bake in greased loaf pan for 1 hour or until loaf tests done. Slice and serve with whipped cream cheese.

Yield: 1 loaf

BLOSSOM CORN BREAD

12	ounces corn muffin mix
8	ounces sour cream
2	eggs
1	(8 ounce) can whole yellow corn, drained
1	(8 ounce) can cream style corn
½	cup butter, room temperature

Preheat oven to 350°. Mix all ingredients well. Pour into greased, 13x9-inch pan and bake for 50 minutes.

Yield: 12 servings

BUBBLE BREAD

1	cup chopped pecans
1	package frozen roll dough
1	package butterscotch pudding (not instant)
½	cup butter
¾	teaspoon cinnamon
1	cup dark brown sugar

Sprinkle pecans in bottom of greased Bundt pan. Add frozen rolls. Sprinkle with pudding mix.Melt butter; add cinnamon and sugar and mix well. Pour over the rolls; cover with plastic wrap and let rise over-night. Bake in preheated 350° oven for 30 minutes.

Yield: 8 to 10 servings

BOSTON BROWN BREAD

½	cup hot water	½	cup brown sugar
1	box raisins	2	teaspoons vanilla
3	tablespoons baking soda	1	teaspoon salt
4	tablespoons butter	4	cups all-purpose flour
1	cup white sugar	2	eggs, well beaten

Preheat oven to 350°. In a large bowl, pour hot water over raisins. Stir in baking soda and mix well. Add butter while still hot. Add white and brown sugars and vanilla. Add salt and flour. Add eggs and mix well. Pour into greased cans until half full. Place on cookie sheet and bake for 45 minutes for soup cans; 55 minutes for bean cans; 65 minutes for coffee cans. Cool before removing from cans.

 Great for gifts!

Yield: 9 soup cans or 6 bean cans or 3 one-pound coffee cans

LEMON-PECAN BREAD

¾	cup softened butter	¼	teaspoon salt
1½	cups sugar	¾	cup buttermilk
3	eggs	¾	cup chopped pecans
2¼	cups self-rising flour	1	teaspoon grated lemon
1	teaspoon baking soda		rind

Preheat oven to 350°. Cream butter. Gradually add sugar, beating well. Add eggs, one at a time, beating well after each addition. Mix flour, baking soda, and salt. Add to creamed mixture alternately with buttermilk, beginning and ending with flour mixture. Stir in pecans and lemon rind. Pour batter into a greased and floured loaf pan. Bake for 1 hour and 15 minutes. Cool thoroughly before removing from pan.

Yield: 1 loaf

PUMPKIN NUT BREAD

1½	cups sifted flour	1	cup mashed pumpkin
1¼	teaspoons baking soda	1	cup sugar
1	teaspoon salt	½	cup buttermilk
1	teaspoon ground	1	egg
	cinnamon	2	tablespoons soft butter
½	teaspoon ground nutmeg	1	cup chopped pecans or
½	teaspoon ground ginger		walnuts

Preheat oven to 350°. Sift together flour, baking soda, salt and spices. Combine pumpkin, sugar, buttermilk and egg in mixing bowl. Add dry ingredients and butter; beat until well blended. Stir in nuts. Spread in well greased loaf pan. Bake for 1 hour or until toothpick inserted in center comes out clean.

Yield: 1 loaf

BRAIDED BREAD

Bread

½	cup warm water	1	tablespoon salt
2	packages active dry yeast	3	eggs
½	cup lukewarm milk	¼	cup soft butter
¼	cup sugar	7¼	cups flour

Glaze (optional)

| 1 | egg yolk | Sesame seeds |
| 2 | tablespoons water | |

Combine all ingredients. Dust a pastry board lightly with flour and knead dough for 8 to 10 minutes or until smooth and elastic. (Use more or less flour as needed.) Let rise 1 to 2 hours in a warm place. Punch dough down and let rise 30 minutes. On a lightly floured board, divide the dough into 6 parts and form each into a 14-inch long roll. Braid 3 of the rolls together; repeat with the other 3 rolls. Place braids on a greased baking sheet and cover; let rise 50 to 60 minutes.

Prepare glaze by mixing egg yolk, water and sesame seeds together and spread on top of braids. Bake in preheated 425° oven for 30 to 35 minutes.

Yield: 2 loaves

STRAWBERRY BREAD

3	cups flour	3	eggs, beaten	
1	teaspoon baking soda	1	cup vegetable oil	
½	teaspoon salt	10	ounces frozen	
1	tablespoon cinnamon		strawberries, thawed	
2	cups sugar	8	ounces cream cheese	

Preheat oven to 350°. Grease and flour 2 loaf pans. Combine first 5 ingredients and mix well. Combine eggs, oil and strawberries. Add strawberry mixture to dry ingredients. Mix well; pour into pans and bake for 1 hour. Let stand in pans until cool. Serve with cream cheese.

Yield: 2 loaves

ZUCCHINI BREAD

3	eggs	¾	teaspoon nutmeg
1	cup vegetable oil	¼	teaspoon baking powder
¾	cup sugar	2	cups zucchini
2	teaspoons vanilla	1	cup well drained crushed
3	cups sifted flour		pineapple
2	teaspoons baking soda	1	cup chopped dates or
1½	teaspoons cinnamon		raisins
1	teaspoon salt	1	cup chopped pecans

Preheat oven to 350°. Beat eggs, oil, sugar and vanilla until thick. Sift flour, baking soda, cinnamon, salt, nutmeg and baking powder together and add to egg mixture. Shred zucchini and add fruit and nuts to above. Mix well and pour into 2, greased, 9x5-inch loaf pans. Bake for 1 hour or until wooden pick inserted in center comes out clean.

 Freezes beautifully!

Yield: 2 loaves

ZUCCHINI CARROT BREAD

2	cups sugar	1	cup vegetable oil
3	cups flour	3	large eggs
1	teaspoon salt	2	cups finely grated
1	teaspoon baking powder		zucchini
¾	teaspoon nutmeg	1	cup finely grated carrots
1½	teaspoons baking soda	1½	cups finely chopped
1¼	tablespoons cinnamon		pecans

Preheat oven to 350°. Combine all ingredients and mix well. Pour into two ungreased 9x5-inch loaf pans. Bake for 1 hour. Cool slightly and remove to racks.

 This is very good when cut into layers and frosted with cream cheese frosting.

Yield: 2 loaves

BOARD AND BATTEN CHEESE BREAD

1	package active dry yeast	2	tablespoons butter
½	cup lukewarm water	1½	teaspoons salt
2	tablespoons sugar	4	cups all-purpose flour
1	cup nonfat dry milk	8	ounces grated sharp
1	cup water		Cheddar cheese

Dissolve yeast in water. Stir in sugar, milk, water, butter and salt. Stir in 3½ cups flour. Knead on board about 8 minutes, adding flour as needed. Place in buttered bowl and brush with butter. Let rise in warm place for 1½ to 2 hours. Punch down. Roll out in a 12x14-inch rectangle. Sprinkle with cheese and roll up. Cut into 1-inch sections; quarter sections. Divide and fill 2 buttered loaf pans. Cover; let rise again until doubled, about 1 hour. Bake in preheated 325° oven for 25 to 30 minutes.

Yield: 2 loaves

LEIGH HOUSE HERB BREAD

1¼	cups warm water	3	cups sifted flour, divided
1	package active dry yeast	1	teaspoon caraway seeds
2	tablespoons soft shortening	½	teaspoon nutmeg
		½	teaspoon sage
2	teaspoons salt	1	tablespoon melted butter
2	tablespoons sugar		

Dissolve yeast in water. Add shortening, salt, sugar, 1½ cups flour, caraway seeds, nutmeg and sage. Beat 2 minutes at medium speed, or 300 strokes by hand. Add remaining flour and blend with spoon until smooth. Scrape batter from sides of bowl, cover with cloth and let rise in warm place 1½ to 2 hours. Beat batter about 25 strokes and spread evenly in greased loaf pan. Smooth top and pat into shape with floured hand; let rise again about 40 minutes. Bake in preheated 350° oven for 45 to 50 minutes. Remove from pan onto rack. Brush top with melted butter.

Yield: 1 loaf

CHURCH STREET FRENCH BREAD

5	cups warm water	5	pounds flour, as needed
2	packages active dry yeast	2	egg whites, slightly beaten
4	tablespoons sugar		
2	tablespoons salt		

Combine first 4 ingredients; stir until dissolved. Add flour gradually, you may not need the entire amount called for. Knead 10 minutes. Let rise in a warm spot until doubled in bulk. Punch down and knead 3 or 4 times to remove air. Divide into 8 equal pieces. Shape into loaves and place in well-greased pans. Slash tops, brush with egg whites and let rise a second time. Bake in preheated 350° oven for 30 minutes. Remove from pans and cool on racks. Wrap in foil when cool and freeze. To serve, warm in foil for 20 minutes in 350° preheated oven.

Yield: 8 loaves

GREENFIELD BEATEN BISCUITS

4	cups plain flour	1	teaspoon salt
4	tablespoons lard or Crisco	1¼	cups cold water

Preheat oven to 400°. When biscuits are put in, reduce heat to 250°. Mix with hands: flour, butter and lard until mixture looks like cornmeal. Add cold water; knead a few times until dough stays together. It will be stiff. Beat with wooden biscuit blade until it blisters. Beat 300 times for home folks, 500 times for company. If you are fortunate enough to have a beaten biscuit machine, use it! Roll dough out, put a little dry flour on it, then fold it over and roll to height of biscuit you want. Cut out with snuff can and place in oven. It takes about an hour to dry them out. Butter and ham are delicious on them!

 You might hear the "Greenfield Blues" while biscuits are baking!

Yield: 48 biscuits

WESSINGTON HOUSE ROLLS

2	cups tepid tap water	1	egg, beaten
1	tablespoon salt	3	tablespoons melted shortening
6	tablespoons sugar		
1	package active dry yeast	6	cups flour

Mix water, salt, sugar and yeast well. Add egg and shortening. Gradually add flour and knead for 10 minutes. Let rise 1½ to 2 hours. Form rolls and let rise about 40 minutes. Bake in preheated 375° oven for 20 to 25 minutes.

Yield: 4 dozen

SOUTHERN SPOON BREAD

1	cup medium ground white cornmeal	3	eggs
1½	cups boiling water	1	teaspoon salt
1	cup milk	2	teaspoons baking powder
		2	tablespoons butter

Preheat oven to 400°. Scald meal with boiling water and stir until blended; add milk. When cool, add well beaten eggs, salt and baking powder. Put butter in baking dish until smoking hot. Pour batter in and bake for 40 to 45 minutes.

 Batter will be very thin.

Yield: 6 to 8 servings

SANS SOUCI SPOON BREAD

4	cups milk	1	cup self-rising yellow cornmeal
½	cup butter, divided		
1½	teaspoons salt	4	eggs
1	tablespoon sugar		

Preheat oven to 400°. Scald milk in top of double boiler. Add 6 tablespoons of butter, salt and sugar. Slowly stir in cornmeal; continue to stir until cornmeal begins to thicken. Beat eggs well and add to hot mixture, stirring until quite thick. Use remaining 2 tablespoons of butter to thoroughly grease bottom and sides of a 2-quart casserole. Pour mixture into dish and bake for 45 minutes.

Yield: 6 to 8 servings

CORNMEAL BOPS

1	cup medium ground white cornmeal	1	scant cup water
½	teaspoon salt	¼	cup vegetable oil

Preheat oven to 450°. Mix cornmeal and salt. Add ½ cup of water and mix; add another ½ cup water. Mix in oil. Grease cookie sheet well and drop bread to desired size "bops". Bake for 30 minutes.

Yield: 1 dozen

CORNICE CORNBREAD

1	cup plain flour	4	egg whites
3	tablespoons baking powder	1	cup skim milk
3-4	tablespoons sugar	¼	cup olive oil
1	cup cornmeal	1	cup non-fat plain yogurt

Preheat oven to 400°. Mix dry ingredients well. Whisk egg whites, milk, oil and yogurt. Stir into dry ingredients until moistened. Pour into ungreased 7½x11¾-inch pan and bake for 25 to 30 minutes. Cut into squares.

 Bake in ungreased tins if muffins are preferred.

Yield: 1 dozen

THOROUGHGOOD SALLY LUNN

1	package active dry yeast	⅓	cup sugar
¼	cup warm water	3	eggs
1	cup scalded milk	4	cups sifted flour
½	cup butter	1	teaspoon salt

Dissolve yeast in warm water. Cool milk and add yeast. Cream butter and sugar in electric mixer; add eggs, one at a time and mix until well blended. At this point, switch beaters to dough hook or beat by hand. Add flour and salt to creamed mixture, alternately with yeast mixture. Beat until smooth. Cover and let rise until double in bulk. Beat down and pour into well greased Bundt or tube pan. Let rise about 40 minutes. Bake in preheated 350° oven for 45 minutes. Do not over cook!

Yield: 1 Sally Lunn

RECTOR'S STUDY

Nestled at the edge of St. Paul's Churchyard is the small one-room building known as the Rector's Study, conveniently located adjacent to the Rectory. While Samuel Iredell Johnston was rector of St. Paul's (1837-1865), this quaint building, with its large chimney and Greek revival woodwork, was built. Today, the building houses the Episcopal Church Women's Gift Shop.

Soups and Sandwiches

SOUPS AND SANDWICHES

BLUEBERRY BISQUE

2	pints blueberries	A few gratings of nutmeg	
3	tablespoons lemon juice	Very fine granulated	
4	cups water	sugar to taste	
2-3	whole cloves	Plain yogurt	
1	1-inch piece of cinnamon stick	Grated orange peel	

Place blueberries in saucepan with lemon juice, water, cloves, cinnamon and nutmeg. Cover and cook over medium heat until berries are soft. Strain soup and taste; it should be tart. If too tart for your taste, add sugar. Chill thoroughly and serve with yogurt and a sprinkle of orange peel.

Yield: 4 servings

CHILLED ROCKY HOCK CUCUMBER SOUP

1	cucumber	1	cup sour cream
½	avocado	2	tablespoons lemon juice
2	green onions		Salt and pepper to taste
1	cup chicken stock		Paprika to taste

Peel and seed cucumber and avocado. Combine with remaining ingredients; place in blender. Blend until smooth and chill overnight. When serving, garnish each bowl with a cucumber slice.

Yield: 4 to 6 servings

BOLTON'S BRIDGE GAZPACHO

1	(10½ ounce) can chicken broth	2	ripe tomatoes, finely chopped
3	spring onions, chopped with tops	1	large cucumber, finely chopped
	Few sprigs parsley, chopped		Salt and pepper to taste
1	cup sour cream		Toasted slivered almonds

Mix first 3 ingredients in blender on medium high. Add sour cream and blend on low. Remove from blender; add tomatoes, cucumbers, salt and pepper. Chill thoroughly. Serve cold, garnished with almonds.

Yield: 4 servings

GARDEN TOMATO SOUP

4	large tomatoes, peeled	¼	teaspoon pepper
4	scallions, snipped	¼	teaspoon oregano
1	cucumber, sliced	¼	teaspoon garlic powder
½	cup chopped green pepper	¼	teaspoon basil
1	cup chicken broth	1	cup V-8 juice
2	teaspoons sugar	1	lemon, juiced
1	teaspoon salt		Parmesan cheese to taste

Simmer vegetables in broth for 5 minutes. Add remaining ingredients; cover and simmer for 10 minutes. Let cool; place in refrigerator for several hours. Serve cold and sprinkle with Parmesan cheese.

 Better 2 days after it's made!

Yield: 4 to 6 servings

ROSY BEET SOUP

4	medium beets	3	tablespoons lemon juice
3	cups chicken broth		Salt to taste
½	cup sour cream		

Cook beets in water until tender. Peel and combine in blender with broth; blend thoroughly. Add sour cream, lemon juice and salt; blend again and chill overnight. When ready to serve, top each serving with a sprig of parsley.

 This is different and very good. Attractive when served in pretty glass bowls.

Yield: 4 to 6 servings

CHILLED ZUCCHINI SOUP

2	large zucchini, sliced	1	(10½ ounce) can chicken
1	medium green pepper,		broth
	chopped	1	cup plain yogurt
1	medium onion, chopped	½	teaspoon fresh dill
1	tablespoon chopped		
	parsley		

Combine first 5 ingredients; simmer for 20 minutes. Puree in food processor or blender and chill thoroughly, at least 2 hours. When ready to serve, garnish with yogurt, dill and a thin slice of zucchini.

Yield: 4 servings

ASPARAGUS SOUP

2	pounds fresh asparagus	1	teaspoon fresh ground
1	cup cream		pepper
1	cup milk	6	tablespoons butter
2	teaspoons tarragon	6	tablespoons flour
2	cups full-bodied white	6	cups chicken broth
	wine	3	chicken bouillon cubes
		1	tablespoon butter

Trim asparagus, remove tips and set aside. Cover stems with well-salted water and boil 12 to 15 minutes. Drain and puree in food processor. Mix cream, milk and puree; set aside. In small saucepan simmer tarragon, wine and pepper until reduced to 2 tablespoons; set aside. Melt butter; add flour and cook 5 minutes. Add broth and bouillon; simmer 1 minute and add puree mixture. Put a cup of soup mixture into the wine and mix well. Strain and add to soup pot. Sauté asparagus tips in butter and float on top of soup for garnish.

Yield: 8 to 10 servings

ALBEMARLE SOUND CLAM CHOWDER

¼	pound bacon	3	stalks celery, diced
6	cups water	12	large fresh clams or 2
3	medium white potatoes, cubed		(6½ ounce) cans whole baby clams
2	medium yellow onions, diced		Clam juice
			Salt and pepper

Cook, drain and crumble bacon. Add with some of pan drippings to pot of water. Bring to simmer and add potatoes, onions and celery. Simmer about 15 minutes. Cut clams very fine with scissors and add, with juice, to pot. Add salt and pepper to taste. Continue simmering for another 20 minutes, stirring frequently.

   2 large tomatoes, coarsely chopped, can be added if desired.

Yield: 6 to 8 servings

BEECH GROVE CABBAGE SOUP

4	bacon slices	1	teaspoon crushed caraway seeds
¾	cup finely chopped onions		Salt and pepper to taste
¼	cup flour	1	tablespoon white wine vinegar
4	cups chicken broth		
6	cups finely chopped cabbage	½	teaspoon sugar
		1	pint half-and-half cream
½	cup diced carrots	¼	cup finely chopped fresh dill
1⅓	cups diced potatoes		

Cook and crumble bacon. Add onion to bacon grease; cook until wilted. Sprinkle with flour and stir. Add chicken broth, stirring constantly. While simmering, add cabbage, carrots, potatoes, caraway seeds, salt, pepper, vinegar and sugar. Cook for 30 minutes, stirring occasionally. Stir in cream and simmer for 5 more minutes. Sprinkle with dill.

Yield: 8 servings

VEGETABLE BEEF SOUP

3	medium leeks	2	large potatoes, peeled and chopped
1	tablespoon cider vinegar		
1	cup unsalted butter	4	quarts beef stock
2	carrots, peeled and chopped	3	pounds coarsely shredded boiled beef
3	ribs celery, cut in chunks		Salt and ground pepper to taste
1	small yellow squash, chopped		
1	small zucchini, chopped	3	ripe Roma tomatoes, chopped
1	pound rutabagas, peeled and chopped	1	cup cooked chick peas

Cut green tops and root ends from leeks. Cut leeks in half lengthwise and soak in cold water and vinegar to cover for 15 minutes. Rinse, dry and chop. Melt butter in stock pot over low heat. Add leeks, carrots and celery. Sauté until vegetables are limp. Add yellow squash, zucchini, rutabagas, potatoes, stock, beef, salt and pepper. Heat to boiling. Reduce heat and simmer until potatoes and rutabagas are tender, about 20 minutes. Stir in tomatoes and chick peas and simmer for 5 minutes.

 Freezes very well.

Yield: 18 servings (5 quarts)

CHICKEN SOUP

1	tablespoon vegetable oil	2	quarts chicken stock
1	cup diced celery	4	cups diced, cooked chicken
1	cup diced carrots		
1	cup diced onions	½	cup uncooked noodles or rice
1	garlic clove, minced		

Heat oil in stock pot. Add celery, carrots, onions and garlic; cover and cook over low heat for 10 minutes. Add stock. Bring to boil and simmer, uncovered, for 10 minutes. Add chicken and noodles or rice; simmer until tender.

Yield: 6 to 8 servings

CHOWAN CORN CHOWDER

3	bacon slices	1	(15 ounce) can stewed	
¼	cup chopped onion		tomatoes	
¼	cup chopped celery		Salt and pepper to taste	
1½	cups diced, cooked potatoes	1	(16 ounce) can cream style corn	
		3	cups milk	

Cut bacon in pieces and fry until crisp. Add onions and celery; sauté until tender. Drain; mix with potatoes and tomatoes. Add salt, pepper, corn and milk. Heat thoroughly but do not boil.

 Substitute 2 8-ounce cans minced clams for corn, and 1 cup clam juice for tomatoes or reduce milk to 2 cups and add ½ cup white wine.

Yield: 6 servings or if multiplied by 6 will serve 50

TOMATO SOUP WITH SOUR CREAM

1	small onion, finely chopped	½	teaspoon thyme	
		½	teaspoon basil	
1	carrot, finely chopped		Salt and pepper to taste	
1	tablespoon butter	1	cup whipping cream	
1	(28 ounce) can Italian style tomatoes, undrained	4	tablespoons sour cream	
		2	teaspoons minced parsley	

Sauté onion and carrot in butter until soft. Add tomatoes, thyme, basil, salt and pepper; bring to boil. Cover, reduce heat, and simmer for 20 minutes. Puree in blender or processor until smooth. Return to pan and add cream. Heat through and serve with 1 tablespoon of sour cream and ½ teaspoon of parsley on top of each serving.

 This soup may also be served cold with the same garnish.

Yield: 4 servings

CREAM OF BROCCOLI SOUP

1	bunch fresh broccoli	2	(10½ ounce) cans
1	onion, chopped		mushroom soup
1	teaspoon nutmeg	1	tablespoon melted butter
1	(10½ ounce) can chicken broth	1	cup sour cream

Cook broccoli, onion and nutmeg in broth until tender. Blend or process until smooth. Mix in soup and butter; add sour cream and blend about 20 seconds. Serve hot with a dollop of sour cream on top.

 May also be served cold.

Yield: 4 servings

CREAM OF MUSHROOM SOUP

1	cup sliced mushrooms	2	cups chicken broth
2	tablespoons chopped onion	1	cup whipping cream
2	tablespoons butter	¼	teaspoon salt
2	tablespoons all-purpose flour	¼	teaspoon nutmeg
		⅛	teaspoon white pepper

Cook mushrooms and onion in butter until tender. Blend in flour and add broth. Cook and stir until slightly thick and bubbly. Stir in cream, salt, nutmeg and pepper. Heat through but be sure not to boil!

Yield: 4 to 6 servings

GREEK LEMON SOUP

6	cups chicken broth	⅛	cup lemon juice
¼	cup uncooked rice	1	lemon, thinly sliced
1	teaspoon garlic salt	2	tablespoons parsley
3	egg yolks		

Bring broth, rice and garlic salt to boil and simmer for 15 minutes. Remove from heat. Beat egg yolks and lemon juice. Ladle a cup of soup into egg mixture and stir. Pour back into soup pot and whisk lightly. Serve hot, using lemon slices and parsley for garnish.

 Use fresh parsley if available.

Yield: 6 servings

QUEEN ANNE CREEK SOUP

1	pound lean ground beef	1	(15 ounce) can string beans, drained
1	large onion, diced		
2	(28 ounce) cans tomatoes	3	tablespoons sugar
2	(15 ounce) cans mixed vegetables		Seasoned salt and pepper to taste
3	bay leaves	2	tablespoons Worcestershire sauce
3	beef bouillon cubes		
1	(3 ounce) can V-8 juice	¼	cup ketchup
¼	cabbage head, diced		Dash of cinnamon or allspice
2	white potatoes, peeled and diced		

Brown beef in large soup pot and drain. Add onion, tomatoes, vegetables, bay leaves, bouillon cubes, V-8 juice, cabbage, potatoes and string beans. Bring to a boil and add sugar and remaining seasonings. Reduce heat and simmer for 1 hour.

 This is a thick soup. Thin with tomato juice as desired.

Yield: 8 to 10 servings

QUICK VEGETABLE SOUP

2	pounds stew beef	1	(8 ounce) package frozen mixed vegetables
1	tablespoon oil		
1	(10½ ounce) can zesty tomato soup	1	(8 ounce) package frozen cut okra
1	(10½ ounce) can vegetable soup	2	cups coarsely chopped cabbage
1	(10½ ounce) can beef broth	1	(15 ounce) can diced tomatoes
4-5	soup cans water	1	ham hock
1	small onion, chopped	1	tablespoon basil
			Salt and pepper to taste

Brown beef in oil. Combine soups and broth with water and stir into browned beef. Add remaining ingredients and simmer for 1 to 2 hours. Remove ham hock before serving.

Yield: 9 to 12 servings

FANTASTIC CARROT SOUP

4	cups chicken stock	⅓	cup sliced almonds
2	pounds chopped carrots	4	tablespoons butter
1½	teaspoons salt	½	cup sour cream
1	medium potato, peeled and chopped	1	teaspoon thyme
		½	teaspoon marjoram
1	cup chopped onion	1½	teaspoons basil
2	garlic cloves, minced		

Bring first 4 ingredients to a boil; lower heat and simmer, covered, for 30 minutes. Sauté onion, garlic and almonds in butter until onions are tender. Puree both mixtures together in blender until very smooth. Heat puree, whisking in sour cream, thyme, marjoram and basil. Serve very hot.

Yield: 5 to 6 servings

GOVERNOR JOHNSTON GUMBO

2	medium onions, chopped	1	tablespoon
1	medium green pepper,		Worcestershire sauce
	chopped	1	quart water
4	stalks celery, chopped	1	bay leaf
2	garlic cloves, minced	¼	teaspoon thyme
1	cup butter, divided	¼	teaspoon basil
3	tablespoons flour		Creole seasoning to taste
2	lemon slices	1	pound crawfish or
			shellfish

Sauté onions, green pepper, celery and garlic in ½ cup melted butter in large kettle until tender. Melt remaining butter in small saucepan; add flour, stirring constantly, and cook until lightly browned, making a roux. Slowly add roux to kettle; add lemon, Worcestershire sauce, water, bay leaf, thyme and basil. Bring to boil; reduce heat to simmer and cook for at least 2 hours. Season with Creole seasoning. Add crawfish or shellfish and cook for 15 minutes. Serve with a side dish of rice.

 Substitute cooked, chopped chicken for seafood.

Yield: 4 to 6 servings

BASE ROAD NAVY BEAN SOUP

1	pound dried navy beans	2	tablespoons finely
8	cups water		chopped parsley
2	cups diced cooked ham	1	teaspoon salt
1	cup finely chopped celery	¼	teaspoon pepper
1	onion, finely chopped	1	bay leaf

Boil beans gently in water for 2 minutes; remove from stove and let stand for 1 hour. Pour into slow cooker. Add remaining ingredients. Cover and cook on low for 12 to 14 hours or until beans are very soft. Remove bay leaf.

 Beans may be soaked overnight if preferred.

Yield: 6 to 8 servings

LIME AND TORTILLA SOUP

2	corn tortillas	1	cup chopped, cooked
	Oil for frying		chicken
2	teaspoons vegetable oil		Salt to taste
⅓	cup chopped onion	2	tomatoes, chopped
½	cup chopped green chilies	1	tablespoon lime juice
4	cups chicken broth	4	large lime slices

Cut tortillas in 2x½-inch strips. Lightly fry tortilla strips in oil ½-inch deep. Drain; set aside. Heat vegetable oil in a large saucepan. Add onion and chili. Sauté until onion is tender but not browned. Add broth, chicken and salt to taste. Cover and simmer 20 minutes. Add tomatoes; simmer 5 minutes longer. Stir in lime juice. Taste and add more lime juice if desired. To serve, ladle soup into bowls and add some fried tortilla strips. Float a lime slice in the center of each serving.

 Good and different!

Yield: 4 servings

BEVERLY HALL BRUNSWICK STEW

2	4-5 pound hens	3	(8 ounce) packages baby
3½	pounds chopped onions		butter beans
6	(16 ounce) cans tomatoes	3½	pounds potatoes
2	(16 ounce) cans white	¼	bottle Worcestershire
	shoepeg corn, drained		sauce
1	(16 ounce) can cream style		Tabasco sauce to taste
	corn		Salt and pepper to taste

Cover hens with water and cook until they begin to fall apart, about 2 hours. Remove bones; add onions and tomatoes, cover, and simmer until cooked to pieces! (This takes several hours on low heat.) Add both cans of corn. Cook butter beans; add to stew. Cook potatoes in boiling water; drain, mash with fork, and add to stew. Simmer for about 1 hour. Stir frequently because it will stick very easily. Taste and adjust seasonings.

 This freezes very well. Let stand in refrigerator overnight before putting in containers.

Yield: 12 to 14 servings

MOUNT AUBURN APPLE SOUP

6	red apples	½	cup butter
6	tart yellow apples	6	(10½ ounce) cans chicken
2	cups chopped onions		broth
2	teaspoons minced garlic		Salt and pepper to taste
	cloves	3	cups whipping cream

Peel, core, and slice apples. Sauté apples, onions and garlic in butter for 5 minutes, stirring occasionally. Add stock, salt and pepper; cook until apples are tender. Add cream and serve.

 Red Delicious and Granny Smith apples are best.

Yield: 8 to 10 servings

EDEN STREET EGGDROP SOUP

6	cups chicken stock	¼	teaspoon white pepper
3	tablespoons cold water	3	eggs, beaten
3	tablespoons cornstarch	4	green onions, diced with
½	teaspoon sugar		tops
1	teaspoon salt		

Heat stock to boiling. Slowly add cold water to cornstarch, mixing until smooth; add sugar, salt and pepper. Stir slowly into stock until smoothly blended. Bring back to boil and immediately reduce heat. Add eggs; stir just a minute until eggs separate. Serve sprinkled with green onions.

 Good for what ails you and only takes a few minutes!

Yield: 6 servings

RUM, POTATO AND AVOCADO SOUP

6	tablespoons butter	6	cups milk
3	tablespoons flour	2	cups mashed potatoes
1	onion, grated	1	tablespoon white rum
2	teaspoons salt	1	avocado, peeled and
½	teaspoon pepper		sliced

Melt butter in saucepan; add flour and onion. Cook, stirring, until begins to brown; season with salt and pepper. Scald milk in double boiler. Add flour/onion paste and potatoes and cook over boiling water, stirring constantly, until mixture becomes the consistency of cream. Just before serving, add rum. Float a slice of avocado in each piping hot soup bowl.

Yield: 6 bowls or 12 cups

SHE-CRAB SOUP

1	cup butter	1	tablespoon parsley
1½	cups flour	2	cups chicken broth
1	half gallon plus 2 cups milk	1	cup dry sherry
		1	(2 ounce) jar pimientos
2	teaspoons salt	1	pound lump crabmeat
1	teaspoon pepper		

Melt butter, add flour and stir until smooth. Gradually add milk, stirring constantly, until it makes a white sauce. Stir in salt, pepper and parsley. In a separate pan cook broth, sherry, pimientos and crabmeat for 5 minutes. Stir into white sauce and serve.

Yield: 8 servings

CRABMEAT SOUP

1	(10½ ounce) can cream of mushroom soup	1½	soup cans milk
1	(10½ ounce) can cream of asparagus soup	1	cup half-and-half cream
		1	pound crabmeat

Blend soups and milk until smooth over medium heat in large saucepan. Stir in cream and crabmeat. Heat through, but do not boil!

Yield: 4 servings

SHRIMP BISQUE

10	large shrimp	2	garlic cloves, crushed
½	cup fish stock or clam juice	¼	cup cognac or brandy
¼	cup unsalted butter	1¾	cups whipping cream
1	cup chopped parsley	10	peppercorns
2	large carrots, chopped	8	fresh tarragon leaves
2	stalks celery, chopped		Ground pepper to taste
2	large shallots, chopped		Pinch of cayenne pepper
		12	snow peas, julienned

Peel and devein shrimp, reserving shells. Halve shrimp lengthwise, cover and refrigerate. Finely chop shrimp shells with stock in processor. Melt butter in heavy saucepan over medium heat. Add parsley, carrots, celery, shallots and garlic; sauté about 5 minutes. Add shell mixture and cook 3 minutes. Add cognac; stir 1 minute. Add cream, peppercorns and tarragon; bring to boil. Reduce heat and simmer until soup is reduced to thin sauce consistency, stirring occasionally, about 10 minutes. Season with cayenne. Strain soup through fine sieve into bowl, pressing on solids with back of spoon. Cover and refrigerate. (Can be prepared a day ahead to this point.) Preheat oven to 350°. Butter 2 deep ovenproof soup bowls. Divide shrimp and half of snow peas between bowls. Bring soup to simmer and pour into bowls. Bake until shrimp are just opaque, about 5 minutes. Scatter remaining snow peas over and serve.

 Worth the trouble!

Yield: 2 servings

CHEESY CHUTNEY OPEN FACE SANDWICH

¼	cup chutney	1	teaspoon Worcestershire
8	ounces soft cream cheese		sauce
	Several teaspoons milk		Green onions, chopped
1	tablespoon curry powder		Paprika

Combine ingredients and chill for 2 hours. Spread on your favorite bread and garnish with chopped green onions and paprika.

 Great for luncheons. Cut bread into fancy shapes.

Yield: 1½ cups

PIMIENTO CHEESE SANDWICHES

12	ounces extra-sharp	½	teaspoon salt
	Cheddar cheese	½	teaspoon ground pepper
1	(4 ounce) jar pimientos,	½	teaspoon seasoned salt
	undrained	½	cup mayonnaise

Grate cheese and pimientos in food processor. Remove to bowl and add remaining ingredients. Serve on whole wheat bread.

 Keeps 1 week, stored in air-tight jar, in refrigerator.

Serve on crackers as hors d'oeuvre.

Yield: About 1 quart

SWISS, BACON AND CRAB SANDWICHES

4	bacon slices	¼	teaspoon pepper
¼	cup mayonnaise	½	pound crabmeat
¼	cup sour cream	½	cup sliced green onions
1	teaspoon Dijon mustard	2	cups grated Swiss cheese
1	teaspoon lemon juice	4	split English muffins
½	teaspoon garlic salt		

Cook, drain and crumble bacon. Mix all ingredients and spread on muffins. Broil 6 inches from heat for 5 minutes or until golden brown.

Yield: 8 servings

CRAB CAKE SANDWICHES

⅓	cup chopped onion	½	teaspoon Old Bay
⅓	cup chopped celery		seasoning
1	tablespoon oil	¼	teaspoon ground red
1½	pounds lump crabmeat		pepper
1	cup soft breadcrumbs	2	tablespoons tartar sauce
1	egg	2	teaspoons mayonnaise
2	tablespoons mayonnaise	8	hamburger buns
2	teaspoons Dijon mustard	8	curly leaf lettuce leaves
2	teaspoons Worcestershire	8	tomato slices
	sauce		Ground pepper to taste

Sauté onion and celery in hot oil until tender. Combine with crabmeat and next 7 ingredients in medium bowl; stir gently until blended. Shape mixture into 8 patties. Place on baking sheet; cover and chill for 15 minutes. Spray a skillet with cooking spray; heat to medium and add crab cakes, cooking until lightly browned on each side. Mix tartar sauce with mayonnaise and spread 1 teaspoon of mixture on one side of each bun; top with 1 crab cake. Top each with a lettuce leaf, tomato slice, ground pepper, and remaining half of hamburger bun. Serve hot.

Yield: 8 servings

OPEN FACE BOULEVARD SANDWICH

Sandwich

1	slice rye bread	2	slices ripe tomato
	Lettuce	2	strips cooked bacon
1	slice Swiss cheese		Hard-boiled egg slices
3	slices cooked chicken		Parsley

Dressing

1	pint mayonnaise	1	teaspoon paprika
¼	cup chili sauce	¼	cup sweet relish
½	cup ketchup	½	cup chopped green
1	teaspoon Worcestershire		pepper
	sauce	1	teaspoon grated onion

Layer sandwich ingredients in order given.

Mix dressing ingredients until well blended and ladle onto sandwiches.

 Dressing is enough for 6 to 8 sandwiches.

Yield: 1 sandwich

BROILED REUBEN SANDWICH

	Butter	6	slices Swiss cheese
12	slices rye bread	12	slices corned beef
½	cup mayonnaise	1	(16 ounce) can sauerkraut
1	tablespoon chili sauce		

Butter one side of each slice of bread and spread a mixture of mayonnaise and chili sauce on the other side. Arrange cheese, beef and sauerkraut on mayonnaise mixture. Put sandwiches together and place on a cookie sheet. Broil each side until brown.

Yield: 6 servings

TANGY VEGETABLE SANDWICH

1	envelope unflavored gelatin	½	cup finely chopped celery
		½	cup finely chopped onion
¼	cup cold water	1	tablespoon lemon juice
1	cup peeled and diced cucumbers	¼	teaspoon salt
		¾	cup mayonnaise
1	cup grated carrots		

Sprinkle gelatin over cold water and place bowl in hot water to dissolve. Combine remaining ingredients and add gelatin, mixing well. Refrigerate until set. Make finger sandwiches with rye or wheat bread.

 Processor can be used for the chopping, just don't overdo!

VIDALIA ONION SPREAD

6	medium Vidalia onions, thinly sliced	2	cups water
		½	cup mayonnaise
½	cup cider vinegar	1	teaspoon celery salt
1	cup sugar		

Mix together onions, vinegar, sugar, and water; marinate 4 hours or overnight. Drain well; mix with mayonnaise and celery salt. Serve on toasted bread with tomato and lettuce.

 Can be served as an hors d'oeuvre on melba rounds.

Yield: 25 servings

CUPOLA HOUSE

The crown of the Edenton tour is a visit to the 1758 Cupola House and garden. A National Historic Landmark, the house is the finest example of Jacobean architecture in the South. Francis Corbin, a sea captain and an agent of Lord Granville, built the house. He included the cupola on the third floor to give himself an unobstructed view as his ships navigated Edenton Bay.

The house is situated among splendidly reconstructed 18th century gardens. The landscape design includes a formal garden in the front and a kitchen herb garden in back.

The Cupola House and its grounds are treasured by Edentonians and enjoyed by everyone.

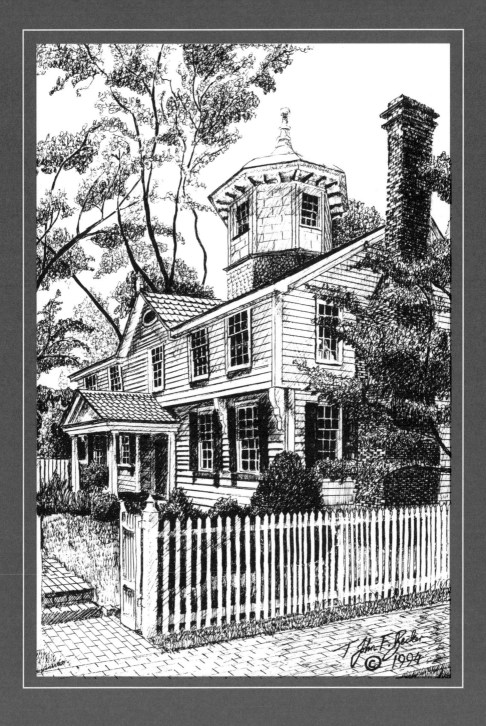

Salads and Salad Dressings

SALADS AND SALAD DRESSINGS

MAINLINE MARINATED ASPARAGUS

1	pound fresh asparagus	¼	teaspoon celery seed
1/3	cup vinegar	½	teaspoon salt
¼	cup sugar	3	whole cloves
¼	cup water	1	stick cinnamon

Blanch asparagus; set aside. Bring vinegar, sugar, water, celery seed, salt, cloves and cinnamon to a boil. Boil about 5 minutes. Remove cloves and cinnamon and pour over asparagus. Cover and refrigerate for 24 hours.

 This is delicious!

Yield: 6 servings

BARROW BROCCOLI SALAD

Salad

1	bunch broccoli	1	cup grated Cheddar
8	bacon slices		cheese
¼	cup sliced red onion	¼	cup sunflower seeds
¼	cup raisins		

Dressing

| 1 | cup Hellmann's | ¼ | cup sugar |
| | mayonnaise | 2 | tablespoons vinegar |

Cut broccoli into florets. Fry bacon and crumble. Add to broccoli along with onion, raisins, cheese and sunflower seeds. Refrigerate until ready to serve.

Mix mayonnaise, sugar and vinegar; refrigerate. Pour dressing over salad just before serving.

Yield: 6 to 8 servings

BEAR SWAMP CAULIFLOWER AND BROCCOLI SALAD

1	head cauliflower	1	tablespoon sugar
1	bunch broccoli	1	teaspoon salt
1	medium onion, chopped	½	teaspoon ground pepper
1	cup mayonnaise	1	tablespoon vinegar

Cut cauliflower and broccoli into florets; add onion. Mix mayonnaise, sugar, salt, pepper and vinegar. Add to vegetables and toss. Cover and chill up to 2 days.

 ½ cup equals 49 calories.

Yield: 12 servings

LAYERED SALAD WITH SPRING ONIONS

1	head lettuce	1½	cups mayonnaise
1	cup chopped celery	2	teaspoons sugar
1	small bunch spring onions, chopped	1	cup grated Parmesan cheese
1	(15 ounce) can LeSueur peas, drained		

Shred lettuce; add celery, onions and peas. Combine mayonnaise and sugar; spread over salad. Sprinkle with Parmesan cheese and serve.

Yield: 6 to 8 servings

GREEN BEANS AND SOUR CREAM SALAD

1¼	cups mayonnaise	1	medium onion, grated
4	teaspoons anchovy paste	2	cups sour cream
8	teaspoons vinegar		Salt and pepper to taste
4	teaspoons lemon juice	8	(15 ounce) cans Blue Lake
1	teaspoon accent		green beans, well drained
2	teaspoons garlic powder		

Combine first 9 ingredients and mix until well blended; pour over beans. Refrigerate overnight.

Yield: 24 servings

PICNIC BEANS

Salad

1	(16 ounce) can Blue Lake green beans, drained	4-6	ounces pickled mushrooms
1	(16 ounce) can kidney beans, drained	1	(16 ounce) can garbanzo beans, drained
2	(6 ounce) jars marinated artichoke hearts, drained	1	(2 ounce) jar chopped pimientos, drained
12	pitted ripe olives	1	tablespoon capers
1	small red onion, thinly sliced	¼	cup chopped parsley
		1	tablespoon chopped green onion

Dressing

½	cup olive oil		Salt and ground pepper to taste
¼	cup herb vinegar		
¼	teaspoon crushed tarragon Pinch of cayenne pepper	1	garlic clove, minced

Combine all the salad ingredients together in large bowl.

Combine dressing ingredients in blender and mix well. Pour dressing over salad and toss gently until blended. Marinate overnight in refrigerator.

 Keeps well for a week or so stored in refrigerator, tightly covered.

Yield: 10 to 12 servings

CUCUMBER AND FETA CHEESE SALAD

2	tablespoons lemon juice Ground pepper to taste	6	ounces crumbled feta cheese
3	tablespoons olive oil	½	cup chopped green onions
2	cucumbers		

Whisk lemon juice and pepper together in a bowl. Add oil slowly, whisking until emulsified. Peel, seed and slice cucumbers; stir into oil mixture along with cheese and onions. Serve on lettuce leaves.

Yield: 6 servings

GREEN BEAN AND BROCCOLI SALAD

1	bunch broccoli	1	cup chopped green onions
1	pound green beans	2	garlic cloves, minced
½	cup olive oil	3	tablespoons finely
⅓	cup lemon juice		chopped mint, lemon
	Salt and ground pepper to		balm or parsley
	taste	½	teaspoon dried hot pepper
3	ounces black olives,		flakes
	pitted and chopped		

Remove florets from broccoli and blanch in boiling water for 2 to 3 minutes. Drain and refresh under cold water. Repeat procedure with beans, cooking for 5 to 7 minutes until crunchy. Place beans and broccoli in serving dish; mix with olive oil and lemon juice. Season with salt and pepper; top with remaining ingredients. Serve at room temperature.

Yield: 8 to 10 servings

WINTER BEAN SALAD

1	(16 ounce) can black beans	2	(3 ounce) cans sliced black olives
1	(16 ounce) can kidney beans	1	(4 ounce) can chopped jalapeño peppers
1	(16 ounce) can navy beans	½	(8 ounce) bottle Italian
1	sweet red pepper, finely diced		dressing

Drain beans and rinse in colander. Mix first 6 ingredients and toss with dressing until well blended. Marinate overnight.

 Best served with grilled chicken.

Yield: 8 to 10 servings

ORIENTAL SALAD

1	cup sugar	1	cup water chestnuts
¾	cup vinegar	1½	cups chopped celery
1	cup green peas	1	teaspoon salt
1	cup French style green beans	1	onion, thinly sliced Ground pepper to taste
1	cup Chinese vegetables		

Dissolve sugar in vinegar. Mix vegetables and add water chestnuts, celery, salt, onion and pepper. Add vinegar/sugar mixture and toss. Chill and serve.

Yield: 4 servings

PILGRIMAGE PEA SALAD

40	(15 ounce) cans LeSueur peas, no substitute	12	(6 ounce) jars chopped pimientos, drained
40	(16 ounce) cans French style green beans	6	cups sugar
4	bunches celery, chopped	6	cups vinegar
6	medium onions, cut in rings	1½	cups oil Salt and ground pepper to taste

Drain peas and beans well. Combine peas, beans, celery, onions and pimientos in large bowl. Mix sugar, vinegar and oil together; salt and pepper to taste. Pour mixture over vegetables and cover tightly. Refrigerate at least one day ahead.

 Keeps well in refrigerator for 2 to 3 weeks. This salad is served at the St. Paul's Pilgrimage luncheons.

Yield: 250 servings

DILL POTATO SALAD

1	cup Italian dressing	6	new red potatoes
½	cup sour cream	1	cucumber, thinly sliced
1	teaspoon salt	1	cup shredded carrots
½	teaspoon dill weed	1	tablespoon minced chives
	Pepper to taste		

Combine first 5 ingredients and mix well; set aside. Cook and cube potatoes. Combine with cucumber, ¾ cup carrots, chives and dressing mixture. Garnish with remaining carrots. Cover and chill until ready to serve.

Yield: 8 to 10 servings

HOUSEPARTY POTATO SALAD

8-10	medium potatoes	1	teaspoon salt
1½	cups Hellmann's mayonnaise	1	tablespoon prepared horseradish
1	cup sour cream	1	cup fresh chopped parsley
1½	teaspoons celery seed	2	medium onions, minced

Boil unpeeled potatoes. Cool; peel and slice thin. Mix mayonnaise, sour cream, celery seed, salt and horseradish; set aside. Combine parsley and onion in small bowl; set aside. Place layer of potatoes in large bowl in which you plan to serve salad. Salt lightly and spread a layer of sour cream/mayonnaise mixture over potatoes, then a layer of onion mixture. Continue layering, as above, ending with onion mixture. Do not stir. Refrigerate, covered, overnight.

 May substitute new red potatoes with skins.

Yield: 10 to 12 servings

SUMMERTIME GREEK SALAD

3	large cucumbers	3	tablespoons olive juice
3	large tomatoes	½	pound Feta cheese, sliced
1	bunch green onions, chopped	8	tablespoons olive oil
		1	teaspoon oregano
10-15	Kalamata olives, seeded and chopped		

Chop cucumbers and tomatoes into large pieces. Add remaining ingredients, toss together and serve at room temperature or chilled.

 Great summer salad!

Yield: 8 servings

ASPARAGUS ASPIC

2	envelopes unflavored gelatin	½	cup chopped celery
1½	cups water	1	(3 ounce) can pimientos
½	cup white vinegar	1	can asparagus spears, undrained
1	cup sugar	1	tablespoon chopped onion
½	teaspoon salt		

Soften gelatin in cool water. Mix remaining water, vinegar, sugar and salt and bring to a boil. Add gelatin mixture and stir until clear. Remove from heat and add celery, pimientos, asparagus and onion. Place in a 9x13-inch casserole and refrigerate until set. Serve over lettuce.

Yield: 12 servings

BING CHERRY SALAD

1	(16 ounce) can pitted Bing cherries	1	(3 ounce) package cherry gelatin
¼	cup water	¾	cup port wine

Drain cherries, reserving juice. Add water to juice to make 1 cup. Bring juice to a boil; remove from heat. Add cherry gelatin and stir until dissolved. Add wine and chill until slightly thickened; add cherries. Return to refrigerator to set.

Yield: 6 servings

CRANBERRY SALAD MOLD

1   (3 ounce) package red
    gelatin
1   cup water
1   (16 ounce) can whole
    cranberry sauce
¾   cup pineapple juice

½   cup diced apples
½   cup chopped celery
1   cup chopped nuts
½   cup whipping cream
1   cup mayonnaise

Dissolve gelatin in boiling water. Add cranberry sauce and pineapple juice and chill until it begins to thicken. Fold in apples, celery and nuts. Pour into sprayed mold and chill. Whip cream, mix in mayonnaise and serve on top of chilled salad.

Yield: 6 to 8 servings

GRAPEFRUIT ASPIC

2   (3 ounce) packages lemon
    gelatin
1½ cups water
2   (9 ounce) cans grapefruit,
    undrained

1   (9 ounce) can crushed
    pineapple, drained
½   cup slivered almonds

Dissolve gelatin in boiling water. Break up grapefruit and add with juice. Add pineapple and almonds. Chill well and serve on a bed of lettuce.

Yield: 1 large ring or 12 individual molds

TOMATO ASPIC

1   envelope unflavored
    gelatin
¼   cup cold water
6   cups V-8 juice

3   (3 ounce) packages lemon
    gelatin
1   cup diced celery

Soften gelatin in cold water. Heat 3 cups V-8 juice in medium sauce-pan. Stir in lemon gelatin until dissolved. Add gelatin to juice mixture and stir well. Add remaining juice and diced celery. Pour into 1-quart mold; refrigerate until set.

Yield: 6 to 8 servings

LITTLEJOHN HOUSE SALAD

1	(15 ounce) can tart pie cherries	½	cup sugar
1	(15 ounce) can crushed pineapple	1	(3 ounce) package lemon gelatin
1	envelope unflavored gelatin		Pinch of salt
¾	cup water	1	grated lemon rind
		1	grated orange rind

Drain fruit and save juice; set fruit aside. Soften unflavored gelatin in ¼ cup fruit juice. Boil remaining juice with water, sugar, lemon gelatin, softened gelatin and salt until all is dissolved. Remove from heat; set aside to cool. When cool, add cherries, pineapple and grated lemon and orange rinds. Pour into 4 to 6-cup mold or into individual molds and chill until firm.

Yield: 6 to 8 servings

VIOLETS WALDORF

3	cups diced apples	¾	cup violets
1¼	cups diced celery	½	cup mayonnaise
¾	cup slivered almonds	½	cup whipping cream
	Sugar to taste		

Combine first 5 ingredients and mix well. Blend mayonnaise and whipping cream together and pour over apple mixture. Serve on bed of lettuce and sprinkle additional violets over each serving.

Yield: 8 servings

ICED CRANBERRY SALAD

2	(16 ounce) cans whole cranberry sauce	2	cups sour cream
2	(7 ounce) cans crushed pineapple	1	cup chopped pecans

Do not drain cranberry sauce or pineapple. Mix all ingredients together and stir well. Pour into 2-quart salad mold and freeze.

Yield: 4 to 6 servings

ROSE-CHAMPAGNE MOLD

2	tablespoons unflavored gelatin	8-12	rosebuds
½	cup water	3-4	cups seedless white grapes
½	cup sugar		Mint leaves
3¼	cups champagne at room temperature		

Soften gelatin in cool water. Place over low heat; stir until dissolved. Stir in sugar until dissolved. Remove from heat and combine with champagne; refrigerate until slightly thickened. Pour about ½ cup of gelatin mixture into a 2-quart ring mold and arrange four rosebuds in inverted positions so they will be upright when unmolded. Chill until firm. Combine 3 cups of grapes and remaining rosebuds with remaining gelatin mixture. Pour ½ cup of grape/gelatin mixture into mold, being careful not to disturb roses. Let it set and then add remainder. When firm, unmold on mint leaves or place mint leaves around outside. Fill center of mold with grapes and serve.

For easy unmolding, rinse a 2-quart ring mold with cold water, shake out droplets, and refrigerate mold until ready to fill.

This recipe was included in the Time/Life series, The Good Cook Salads.

Yield: 12 servings

FROZEN FRUIT SALAD

2	cups sour cream	3	tablespoons minced cocktail cherries with juice
1	banana, diced		
1	(9 ounce) can crushed pineapple	⅓	cup chopped pecans
		¾	cup sugar
		2	tablespoons lemon juice

Mix all ingredients and pour into paper-lined muffin tins. Freeze. When frozen, remove from tins and place in freezer bags. Remove from freezer as needed; partially thaw and garnish with yogurt or cream.

Add other fruits of personal choice or whatever is in season.

Yield: 12 servings

BOOTH HOUSE SALAD

Salad

6	cups assorted lettuces and Radicchio	¼	pound crumbled goat cheese

Dressing

1	tablespoon Dijon mustard	5	tablespoons olive oil
2	tablespoons Balsamic vinegar		Salt to taste
1	tablespoon chopped fresh garlic		Lots of freshly ground pepper

Toss Radicchio with goat cheese; set aside.

Combine mustard, vinegar and garlic; then, whisking constantly, add olive oil in steady stream. Add salt and pepper. Pour over salad and toss.

 This is a great salad to serve with beef or lamb.

Yield: 6 servings

COBB SALAD

1	large avocado, diced	⅛	teaspoon freshly ground pepper
1	tablespoon lemon juice		
1	medium head iceberg lettuce	3	tablespoons chopped chives
2	hard-boiled eggs	½	cup salad oil
1	pound bacon	1	large tomato, diced
6	tablespoons white wine vinegar	1½	cups diced cooked chicken
½	teaspoon salt	3	ounces crumbled blue cheese
⅛	teaspoon garlic powder		

Peel avocado and toss with lemon juice; set aside. Shred lettuce in large wide salad bowl. Chop eggs. Cook and crumble bacon. In a jar combine vinegar, salt, garlic powder, pepper, chives and oil. Shake well and pour over lettuce and toss. Arrange in wedge-shaped sections on top of lettuce the tomato, avocado, eggs, chicken and bacon. Place blue cheese in center. Toss together at the table and serve.

Yield: 4 to 6 servings

CAESAR SALAD

1	garlic clove	½	teaspoon fresh ground
1	egg		pepper
½	cup grated Parmesan	½	teaspoon salt
	cheese	½	cup olive oil
4	tablespoons lemon juice	1-2	heads Romaine lettuce
1	tablespoon	¾	cup croutons
	Worcestershire sauce		

Put first 7 ingredients in blender and blend until smooth. With blender running, add oil in slow, steady stream until emulsified. Place torn Romaine in bowl and top with dressing. Toss and add croutons.

Yield: 4 to 6 servings

BLUE CHEESE SLAW

2	pounds shredded cabbage	½	teaspoon garlic salt
¾	cup mayonnaise		Large pinch sugar
¼	cup lemon juice		Ground pepper to taste
¼	cup vinegar	½	cup crumbled blue cheese

Place cabbage in bowl. In another bowl, whisk together remaining ingredients; pour over cabbage. Refrigerate for 2 hours and serve.

Yield: 8 servings

VILLAGE GREEN SLAW

1	green pepper, chopped	1	teaspoon salt
1	cabbage, chopped	¾	cup oil
1	onion, chopped	1	teaspoon dry mustard
1	cup sugar	1	teaspoon celery seed
1	cup vinegar		

Mix pepper, cabbage and onion; set aside. Bring remaining ingredients to a boil and pour over cabbage mixture. Let stand in refrigerator until well chilled, about 2 to 3 hours.

Yield: 6 to 8 servings

HOT CHICKEN SALAD

4	cups diced cooked chicken	1	teaspoon minced onion
2	tablespoons lemon juice	1	(3 ounce) jar pimientos
1	cup mayonnaise	1	(4 ounce) can mushrooms, drained
1	teaspoon salt	1	cup grated sharp Cheddar cheese
2	cups chopped celery		
2	hard-boiled eggs, coarsely chopped	1	cup chopped pecans
1	cup cream of chicken soup	1	cup crushed potato chips

Preheat oven to 400°. Mix first 10 ingredients and place in a 9x13-inch casserole. Mix cheese, pecans and potato chips together and spread on top. Bake for 25 minutes.

Yield: 12 servings

ST. PAUL'S PILGRIMAGE CHICKEN SALAD

24	large chickens	2	tablespoons Jane's Crazy Salt
1	(8 ounce) bottle lemon juice	2	tablespoons ground pepper
4	bunches celery	5½	quarts mayonnaise
2	tablespoons dill weed		Paprika
2	tablespoons Mrs. Dash		
2	tablespoons salt		

Cook, bone and cube chicken. Mix all ingredients, except mayonnaise and paprika, the day before serving; refrigerate to let flavors marinate. Mix with mayonnaise the next morning. Serve on a bed of lettuce and sprinkle with paprika.

 The Episcopal Church Women serve this salad at the Biennial Pilgrimage luncheon at St. Paul's.

Yield: 175 servings

SESAME CHICKEN SALAD

2	tablespoons sesame seeds	2	teaspoons minced fresh ginger
¼	cup salad oil		
3	tablespoons lemon juice	½	pound pea pods
1½	tablespoons soy sauce	½	pound bean sprouts
1½	tablespoons white wine vinegar	3½	cups chopped, cooked chicken
3	garlic cloves, minced		

Toast sesame seeds over medium heat, stirring often, about 5 minutes. Place in a serving bowl and add oil, lemon juice, soy sauce, vinegar, garlic and ginger. Set aside. Drop peas and sprouts into a 6-quart kettle half filled with boiling water. Cook until water resumes a full boil; drain, rinse well with cold water and drain again. Add vegetables and chicken to sesame mixture and stir gently.

Yield: 4 servings

UPTOWN TURKEY SALAD

Salad

1	6-pound turkey breast, cooked and cubed	½	cup blanched whole almonds
1	bunch radishes	¾	cup chopped scallions
½	cup half-and-half cream	¼	cup chopped parsley
5	stalks celery	½	teaspoon pepper
2	(16 ounce) cans pineapple chunks, drained	1	head of crisp lettuce

Dressing

¼	cup vegetable or olive oil	2	tablespoons fresh tarragon
½	cup lemon juice		

Mix turkey with all salad ingredients except lettuce.

Combine all dressing ingredients; mix well. Toss together salad and dressing; cover and refrigerate until well chilled. Serve on a bed of lettuce.

 Chicken or pork may be substituted for the turkey.

Yield: 12 to 15 servings

TURKEY SALAD PLATE

Salad Plate

4	large lettuce leaves	1	tablespoon chopped
12	turkey breast slices		chives
2	tomatoes, sliced		Black olives
1	(15 ounce) can hearts of palm		

Dressing

3	tablespoons Dijon mustard	¼	cup vinegar
¼	cup oil	¼	cup whipping cream

On 4 salad plates, top lettuce leaf with 3 slices of turkey. Arrange tomato slices and hearts of palm on each plate. Sprinkle with chives and garnish with olives.

Whisk together the dressing ingredients and pour over each salad.

Yield: 4 servings

CHRISTMAS SALAD

1	head lettuce, your choice	8	teaspoons red or black caviar
2	tomatoes		
4	hard-boiled eggs	8	3-inch rounds of toast Russian dressing

Create a bed of lettuce on each plate. Place one toast round on top of lettuce and ¼-inch slice of tomato on top of toast. Remove yolks from egg halves and set aside. Fill half of egg with caviar and place egg, cut side down on tomato. Cover with Russian dressing and garnish with crumbled egg yolk. Repeat process until all salads are completed.

Yield: 8 servings

ROAST BEEF SALAD

1	cucumber, peeled and sliced	1	tablespoon vinegar
1	cup grated Swiss cheese	1	tablespoon prepared horseradish
1	cup cooked, cubed roast beef	1	avocado, peeled and sliced
½	cup sliced green onions	2	tomatoes, sliced
⅔	cup commercial creamy cucumber salad dressing	4	lettuce leaves

Combine first 4 ingredients. Mix dressing with vinegar and horseradish. Pour over beef mixture and chill. Arrange beef, avocado and tomato on lettuce leaves on each plate and serve.

 This is a great way to use up that leftover roast beef.

Yield: 4 servings

EDENTON BAY SEAFOOD SALAD

Salad

½	head Romaine lettuce	½	cup cooked, peeled shrimp
½	head chicory	½	cup crabmeat
½	head iceberg lettuce	1	hard-boiled egg, coarsely chopped
1	cucumber, thinly sliced		
2	tomatoes, quartered	6	ripe olives, sliced
½	cup lobster meat	6	green olives, sliced

Dressing

1	teaspoon paprika	½	teaspoon lemon juice
4	tablespoons olive oil	1	teaspoon salt
½	teaspoon vinegar		Dash of pepper

Mix lettuces with remaining salad ingredients and toss well.

Blend paprika and oil; add vinegar, lemon juice, salt and pepper. Shake in a bottle until blended; pour over salad and toss.

Yield: 4 to 6 servings

CRAB LOUIS

1	cup mayonnaise	1	lemon, juiced
¼	cup chili sauce	2	small heads iceberg
¼	cup finely chopped green		lettuce
	pepper	1	pound crabmeat
¼	cup finely chopped green	4	large tomatoes
	onions	4	hard-boiled eggs
¼	cup whipping cream	1	lemon
	Salt to taste		Parsley to taste

Combine mayonnaise, chili sauce, green peppers and onions. Whip cream and fold into mixture. Season with salt and lemon juice. Arrange outer leaves of lettuce on 4 plates. Shred remaining lettuce and divide evenly among plates. Place crabmeat on top. Cut tomatoes and eggs in wedges and arrange around crab. Spoon dressing over salad and garnish with parsley and lemon wedges.

Yield: 4 servings

SHRIMP AND AVOCADO SALAD

1	large red onion, sliced	2	tablespoons chopped
2	tablespoons tequila		fresh cilantro
½	teaspoon sugar	1	garlic clove, minced
	Salt to taste	1	tablespoon Dijon mustard
16	large shrimp	2	ripe avocados
1	teaspoon chili powder	3	plum tomatoes, finely
4	limes		sliced and cored
6	tablespoons olive oil	2	heads Romaine lettuce
4	Serrano chilies, seeded		
	and finely chopped		

Toss onion with tequila, sugar and a pinch of salt. Allow to stand for 30 minutes, stirring occasionally. Place shrimp, chili powder and juice of 2 limes in a small saucepan; cover with water and bring to a boil. Reduce heat and simmer for 1 minute. Drain shrimp, cool to room temperature, and peel. Combine juice of 1 lime with olive oil, chilies, cilantro, garlic and mustard until mixed thoroughly. Peel, seed and cut avocados into chunks. Toss with tomatoes and shrimp. Gently fold in dressing mixture. Serve on lettuce leaves and garnish with onion and lime slices.

Yield: 4 servings

CHEESY SALAD DRESSING

¾	cup vegetable oil	1	teaspoon white pepper
¼	cup vinegar	½	teaspoon seasoned salt
1	teaspoon accent	8	ounces grated sharp
1	teaspoon granulated		Cheddar cheese
	onion		

Mix all ingredients together until well blended.

 Keeps in refrigerator for several weeks.

Yield: 2 cups

OILS AND VINEGARS DRESSING

¾	cup vegetable oil	3	tablespoons herb wine
¼	cup olive oil		vinegar
4	tablespoons sugar	3	tablespoons basil vinegar
3	tablespoons Balsamic	1	teaspoon salt
	vinegar		Ground pepper to taste
3	tablespoons red wine	2	teaspoons yellow mustard
	vinegar		

Mix all ingredients and stir briskly with a wire whisk. Bottle and store in your cupboard as it does not need to be refrigerated.

 Use any combination of vinegars, but always include Balsamic!

Yield: 2 cups

SPINACH SALAD DRESSING

1	onion, chopped	2	tablespoons brown
¼	cup brown sugar		mustard
½	teaspoon black pepper	¼	cup cider vinegar
1	teaspoon salt	1	cup vegetable oil

Mix all ingredients well and heat slightly. Serve warm or chilled.

Yield: 1½ cups

LIVINGSTON DRESSING

1	cup tomato ketchup	1	teaspoon Worcestershire
⅓	cup olive oil		sauce
¼	cup water		Dash of hot sauce
¼	cup wine vinegar		Dash of ground nutmeg
1	tablespoon sugar		Ground pepper to taste
			Crushed garlic to taste

Mix all ingredients well and pour into bottle. Refrigerate until ready to serve.

Yield: 1½ cups

POPPY SEED DRESSING

⅔	cup white vinegar	2	teaspoons dry mustard
2	teaspoons finely grated	2	teaspoons salt
	onion	2	cups vegetable oil
1	cup sugar	3	tablespoons poppy seeds

Combine vinegar, onion, sugar, mustard and salt. Beat with wire whisk until sugar, salt and mustard dissolve. Beating constantly, slowly pour in oil and beat until dressing is smooth and thick. Stir in the poppy seeds and taste for seasoning. Serve with any fruit salad.

Yield: 2½ cups

BEVERLY HALL

Amble along West King Street and enjoy the house and gardens of Beverly Hall. The house, built around 1810, once served as a branch of the State Bank of North Carolina. A rest on the side porch offers a view of the fountain and Edenton's most highly developed Victorian garden. The restoration of the garden is made possible by the discovery of many historic photographs.

Beverly Hall has served as the home for five generations of the present owner's family.

D. Boyle '91

Pasta

PASTA

BLOUNT STREET BOW TIES

Pasta

16	ounces bow tie pasta
3	tablespoons shredded carrots
½	cup cooked diced ham
½	cup grated Cheddar cheese
3	tablespoons thawed frozen peas

Dressing

¼	cup Parmesan cheese
½	cup whipping cream
1	cup mayonnaise
1	garlic clove, minced
	Salt to taste
	Ground pepper to taste

Cook pasta according to package directions; drain and set aside to cool. Mix carrots, ham, cheese and peas together and toss with cool pasta.

Soften Parmesan cheese in cream for 15 minutes. Stir in mayonnaise, garlic, salt and pepper. Pour over pasta and toss gently.

Yield: 4 to 6 servings

CHILLED TORTELLINI PASTA

2	pounds shrimp
16	ounces cheese tortellini
¾	cup olive oil
¾	cup lemon juice
1	cup basil leaves
2	garlic cloves, minced
½	cup grated Parmesan cheese
	Garlic salt to taste
	Ground pepper to taste

Peel, clean and cook shrimp. Cook tortellini according to package directions; drain and let cool. Combine olive oil, lemon juice, basil, garlic and Parmesan cheese in food processor. Process until mixed well. Toss with tortellini and shrimp; add garlic salt and pepper. Garnish with fresh basil leaves.

Yield: 12 servings

YEOPIM CREEK PASTA SALAD

Pasta

3½	cups cooked macaroni shells	3	cups cooked broccoli florets	
3	chicken halves, cooked and boned	1	cup red pepper strips	
		6	ounces snow peas	
		¼	cup chopped green onions	

Dressing

¼	cup oil	2	garlic cloves, minced	
¼	cup plus 1 tablespoon red wine vinegar	1	teaspoon hot sauce	
2	tablespoons honey	½	teaspoon ground ginger	
2	teaspoons sesame seeds	¼	teaspoon salt	

Combine pasta ingredients and toss until blended; set aside.

Whisk together dressing ingredients and toss with pasta. Chill and serve.

Yield: 4 servings

LAYERED CHICKEN PASTA SALAD

2	cups cooked chicken breasts	1	(8 ounce) package frozen peas	
1	tablespoon lemon juice	1	cup mayonnaise	
½	teaspoon salt	1	cup sour cream	
¼	teaspoon pepper	3	tablespoons Parmesan cheese	
4	cups lettuce			
1	cup celery	1½	cups grated Cheddar cheese	
1	cup cooked pasta			

Chop chicken and combine with lemon juice, salt and pepper. In deep glass bowl, layer lettuce, celery, chicken, pasta and peas. Mix mayonnaise and sour cream and spread completely over peas. Sprinkle with Parmesan, then Cheddar cheese. Cover and chill thoroughly before serving.

 Can use crab or shrimp in place of chicken.

Yield: 4 servings

COURT STREET PASTA

Chicken

3	pounds chicken breasts		2	tablespoons chopped
	Water to cover			parsley
8	ounces vermicelli			Marinated mushrooms
½	bunch broccoli florets			Marinated artichoke
½	cup mayonnaise			hearts
	Leaf lettuce			Cherry tomatoes
				Parsley sprigs

Dressing

¼	cup wine vinegar		½	teaspoon ground pepper
2	teaspoons Dijon mustard		2	tablespoons olive oil
½	teaspoon chopped garlic		2	tablespoons vegetable oil
½	teaspoon salt			

Bring chicken to a boil; reduce heat and simmer 45 minutes or until tender. Remove from heat and cool. Bone and chop chicken in ½-inch chunks; set aside. Cook vermicelli according to package directions, omitting salt; drain.

Combine vinegar, mustard, garlic, salt and pepper; mix well. Gradually add olive oil and vegetable oil; whisk mixture until blended. Toss vermicelli and dressing; add chicken, broccoli and mayonnaise. Mix well and chill at least 1 hour. Spoon pasta mixture into the center of a lettuce-lined platter; sprinkle with parsley. Arrange mushrooms, artichoke hearts and tomatoes around pasta. Garnish with parsley sprigs.

Yield: 4 to 6 servings

FREEMASON NOODLES

8	ounces egg noodles	2	dashes Tabasco sauce
4	tablespoons butter	½	teaspoon salt
1	cup cottage cheese	½	teaspoon garlic salt
1	cup sour cream		Grated fresh Parmesan
2	spring onions, chopped		cheese

Cook noodles according to package directions; drain and toss with butter. Add remaining ingredients and stir gently to combine. Recipe can be frozen at this point or refrigerated overnight. When ready to serve, bake at 350° for 45 minutes.

Yield: 6 to 8 servings

EAST CUSTOMS HOUSE NOODLE CASSEROLE

12	ounces egg noodles	2	(10½ ounce) cans cream of
2	bay leaves		mushroom soup
1	onion, chopped	1	(3 ounce) jar pimientos
1	green pepper, chopped		Grated sharp Cheddar
½	cup mushrooms		cheese
¼	cup butter		

Preheat oven to 350°. Cook noodles with bay leaves according to package directions. Drain and rinse with cold water. Sauté onion, pepper and mushrooms in butter. Add to noodles along with soup and pimientos. Mix well and place in casserole dish; top with cheese. Bake for 40 minutes.

 Tuna or chopped, cooked chicken may be added.

Yield: 8 servings

FETTUCCINE VERDE

6	tablespoons butter	1½	cups grated Parmesan
1	cup sliced green onions		cheese
2	garlic cloves, minced		Salt and pepper to taste
1	cup whipping cream	⅛	teaspoon nutmeg
8	ounces spinach fettuccine		

Melt butter in large frying pan; sauté onions and garlic. Cook a few minutes; add cream. Boil rapidly until slightly thickened. Cook fettuccine according to package directions; drain and toss gently with cream. Add ½ cup of cheese and mix until coated. Add another ½ cup of cheese, salt and pepper. Toss. Sprinkle nutmeg and remaining ½ cup of cheese over the top and serve.

Yield: 4 servings

MADEIRA PASTA

6	tablespoons butter	1½	teaspoons salt
1	medium onion, finely	½	teaspoon pepper
	chopped	½	cup Madeira wine
1	pound mushrooms,	⅔	cup whipping cream
	chopped	8	ounces pasta
3	tablespoons flour		Chopped parsley
3	cups chicken broth		

Melt butter; add onion and sauté 10 minutes. Add mushrooms and cook 2 minutes. Sprinkle in flour and cook until bubbly. Gradually stir in broth and season with salt and pepper. Bring to boil, cover, and simmer 10 minutes. Stir in wine and cream. Heat through but do not boil. Cook pasta according to package directions. Drain and cover with sauce. Garnish with parsley.

Yield: 4 servings

FETTUCCINE WITH SPINACH

8	ounces fettuccine	¼	cup butter
2	tablespoons chopped onion	½	cup whipping cream
1	garlic clove, crushed	1	cup grated Parmesan cheese
1	tablespoon melted butter		Coarsely ground pepper
1	pound fresh spinach		

Cook fettuccine according to package directions; drain and keep warm. Sauté onion and garlic in butter until tender; stir in spinach, cover and simmer 3 minutes. Add ¼ cup butter to warm pasta, tossing gently until butter melts. Add spinach mixture, cream and cheese. Toss gently and sprinkle with pepper.

Yield: 8 servings

A "LITTLE DIFFERENT" SPAGHETTI

1½	pounds lean ground beef	1	(7¼ ounce) bottle stuffed olives, sliced
¼	cup plus 1 tablespoon olive oil		Crushed red pepper to taste
3	small onions, finely diced		Salt and pepper to taste
1	green pepper, finely diced	1	quart tomatoes
2	tablespoons chili powder	½	cup sliced mushrooms
16	ounces cream cheese, cut in chunks	12	ounces spaghetti Parmesan cheese

Preheat oven to 350°. Brown beef in 1 tablespoon of olive oil; add onions and green pepper. Add remaining oil, chili powder and cream cheese, mixing well. Add olives, red pepper, salt and pepper, tomatoes and mushrooms. Simmer for 15 minutes. Cook spaghetti according to package directions. Drain; mix with sauce and put in 9x13-inch casserole. Sprinkle with Parmesan cheese and bake for 45 minutes.

Yield: 10 to 12 servings

LONG BEACH LASAGNA

2	pounds ground beef	1	bay leaf
2	onions, chopped	½	teaspoon oregano
2	garlic cloves, minced	½	teaspoon salt
1	(28 ounce) can whole tomatoes, undrained	¼	teaspoon pepper
		¾	tablespoon parsley
1	(12 ounce) can tomato paste	2	cups cottage cheese
		8	ounces mozzarella cheese
2	(15 ounce) cans tomato sauce	8	ounces Swiss cheese
		16	ounces lasagna noodles
½	pound chopped mushrooms		

Preheat oven to 350°. Brown beef, onions and garlic; add next 9 ingredients, mixing well. Simmer for 30 minutes. Cook lasagna according to package directions; drain. Layer noodles, meat sauce, cottage cheese, mozzarella and Swiss cheese in greased casserole. Repeat layers and bake for 40 minutes.

Yield: 12 servings

PASTA ON A PLATE

2	cups fresh spinach	3	chopped sun-dried tomatoes
2	ounces fettuccine or penne		Parsley, coarsely chopped
2	teaspoons pine nuts		Ground pepper to taste
1	garlic clove, chopped		Wine of choice for the cook
3	tablespoons olive oil		
¼	cup Parmesan cheese		

Coarsely chop spinach and arrange on plate. Place plate on stove to warm while cooking pasta al dente. Toast pine nuts — watch carefully! Sauté garlic in olive oil, but do not brown. Remove from heat and set aside. Slice Parmesan cheese with a vegetable peeler and place on chopping board with tomatoes and parsley. Chop all together; add to sauté pan with pasta. Toss like crazy and pour this delicious smelling concoction on top of spinach. Add lots of ground pepper, have a glass of wine, and enjoy!

 Special evening meal for one.

Yield: 1 serving or multiply for more

PASTA WITH FOUR CHEESES

16	ounces spinach pasta	¼	pound cubed Gorgonzola
1	cup butter	¼	pound cubed Bel Paese
	Salt and pepper to taste	¾	cup grated Parmesan
¼	pound cubed fontina		cheese
	cheese	1	cup whipping cream

Cook pasta according to package directions; drain and keep warm. Melt butter and add first three cheeses. Stir until melted. Stir in Parmesan cheese and cream. Salt and pepper to taste; toss with hot pasta and serve.

 If you cannot find the above cheeses, substitute with saga blue, Boursin, Monterey Jack, etc.

Yield: 6 to 8 servings

LINGUINE WITH CLAM SAUCE

4	garlic cloves, minced	1	tablespoon green pepper, finely chopped
1	medium onion, minced		
¼	cup melted butter		Pinch of red pepper flakes
¼	cup olive oil	2	(6½ ounce) cans clams, with juice
¼	cup chopped fresh parsley		
3	tablespoons Parmesan cheese, grated	1	(8 ounce) can tomato sauce
1	tablespoon dried oregano	8	ounces linguine

Sauté onions in butter; add garlic but do not brown. Add next six ingredients, stirring to combine. Add clams and tomato sauce. Simmer, covered, for 45 minutes to 1 hour. While sauce is cooking, prepare linguine according to package directions. When sauce is done, serve over cooked linguine.

 Excellent Lenten dinner. Serve with French bread and dry white wine.

Yield: 6 servings

PARLOR PASTA PRIMAVERA

2	garlic cloves, minced	4	scallions, finely chopped
3	tablespoons butter	2	carrots, julienned
1	tablespoon oil	1	red pepper, chopped
2	cups broccoli florets	16	ounces rotelli
2	zucchini, chopped		Grated Parmesan cheese

Sauté garlic in butter and oil until golden, about 2 to 3 minutes. Add vegetables; cook until tender and crisp. Cook rotelli according to package directions; drain well and place in dish; toss in vegetables. Top each serving with cheese.

Yield: 4 to 6 servings

SUN-DRIED TOMATOES AND VERMICELLI

1	(3 ounce) package sun-dried tomatoes	½	teaspoon basil
		½	teaspoon salt
18	garlic cloves, peeled	½	teaspoon ground pepper
¾	cup olive oil	¼	cup balsamic vinegar
½	teaspoon oregano	8	ounces vermicelli

Simmer tomatoes in hot water for 20 minutes; drain and squeeze out excess water. Sauté garlic in olive oil until soft; add tomatoes and remaining ingredients, except vermicelli, and cook about 5 minutes. Cook pasta according to package directions; drain. Pour sauce over warm pasta.

 Use in any recipe calling for sun-dried tomatoes packed in oil, omitting pasta. Cover top of block of cream cheese for an hors d'oeuvre.

Yield: 1½ cups

111

PIZZA SPAGHETTI CASSEROLE

8	ounces spaghetti	½	teaspoon basil
1	small onion, chopped	½	teaspoon oregano
⅓	cup butter	8	ounces grated mozzarella
2	(8 ounce) cans tomato		cheese
	sauce	3½	ounces grated Swiss
1	cup sliced mushrooms		cheese
1	garlic clove, minced	6	ounces sliced pepperoni

Preheat oven to 350°. Cook spaghetti according to package directions; drain and set aside. Sauté onion in butter. Add next 5 ingredients and stir to make a sauce. In 9x13-inch casserole, layer half the spaghetti, half the sauce, half the cheese and half the pepperoni. Repeat layers and bake for 25 minutes.

 This is delicious and everyone loves it!

Yield: 6 to 8 servings

SYCAMORE SIDE DISH

8	ounces spaghetti	½	cup water
1	onion, chopped	1	cup sliced mushrooms
2	stalks celery, chopped		Salt and pepper to taste
1	green pepper, chopped	1	teaspoon chili powder
¼	cup olive oil		Grated sharp Cheddar
2	(8 ounce) cans tomato		cheese
	sauce		Parmesan cheese

Preheat oven to 350°. Cook spaghetti according to package directions; drain and set aside. Sauté onions, celery and green pepper in olive oil. Add tomato sauce, water, mushrooms, salt, pepper and chili powder. Cook for about 15 minutes or until sauce thickens. Layer spaghetti, sauce and cheeses. Bake for 25 minutes.

Yield: 6 servings

SPICY LINGUINE

16	ounces linguine	½	cup rice vinegar
3	tablespoons oil	1	tablespoon honey
¾	cup sliced radishes	4	scallions
3	scallions, finely chopped	¼	cup peanut oil
3	garlic cloves, minced	3	tablespoons sesame oil
¼	teaspoon ground ginger	1	teaspoon hot chili oil
1½	teaspoons red pepper flakes	½	cup sesame tahini
			Lemon zest
½	cup soy sauce	¼	cup toasted sesame seeds

Cook pasta according to package directions; drain well and toss with 3 tablespoons oil. Add radishes and scallions; set aside. Combine remaining ingredients (except lemon zest and sesame seeds) in food processor and mix until smooth. Pour over linguine and toss. Refrigerate until chilled, about 3 hours. Bring to room temperature before serving and garnish with lemon zest and sesame seeds.

Yield: 6 servings

SPINACH FETTUCCINE WITH MUSHROOMS AND ARTICHOKES

4	tablespoons olive oil	1	cup whipping cream
1	pound mushrooms, sliced	½	cup milk
3	garlic cloves, pressed	½	cup grated Parmesan cheese
1	teaspoon dried thyme, crumbled		Salt and pepper to taste
1	large red bell pepper, coarsely chopped	16	ounces spinach fettuccine
			Parmesan cheese
1	(14 ounce) can artichoke hearts, drained		

Heat 3 tablespoons oil in large skillet over high heat. Add mushrooms, garlic and thyme; sauté until mushrooms are golden, about 6 minutes. Add pepper; sauté 3 minutes. Add artichoke hearts, cream, milk and cheese; simmer 3 minutes. Season with salt and pepper. Cook fettuccine according to package directions; drain and toss with remaining oil. Cover with sauce and serve with additional cheese on the side.

Yield: 6 servings

SPRINGTIME NOODLES

1	pound chopped mushrooms	3	zucchini, sliced
3	small onions, sliced	8	ounces spinach noodles
3	garlic cloves, minced	1	egg yolk, optional
7	tablespoons melted butter		Salt and pepper to taste
2	cups chopped cooked ham		Grated Parmesan cheese
		⅓	cup sour cream

Cook mushrooms, onions and garlic in 4 tablespoons of butter until soft. Add chopped ham; set aside. Blanch zucchini; set aside. Cook noodles according to package directions. Drain and combine with egg yolk, remaining butter, salt, pepper, Parmesan cheese and sour cream. Combine mushroom/ham mixture, zucchini and noodle/cheese mixture. Toss together and serve.

Yield: 4 to 6 servings

ZUCCHINI LASAGNA

½	pound ground beef	½	teaspoon basil
⅓	cup chopped onion		Pepper to taste
2	tablespoons olive oil	1	egg
1	(15 ounce) can tomato sauce	1	cup cottage cheese
	Salt to taste	4	medium zucchini
½	teaspoon oregano	2	tablespoons flour
		¼	pound mozzarella cheese

Preheat oven to 375°. Brown beef and onion in oil. Spoon off fat; add tomato sauce, herbs and seasonings and bring to boil. Reduce heat and simmer 5 minutes. Mix egg and cottage cheese. Thinly slice zucchini and layer half in a 12x8-inch baking dish; sprinkle with flour. Top with all of cottage cheese mixture and half of meat sauce. Repeat zucchini, flour, mozzarella and meat sauce. Bake, uncovered, for 45 minutes. Let stand for 10 minutes before serving.

 Freezes nicely.

Yield: 4-6 servings

SPAGHETTI PUTTANESCA

24	littleneck clams (the smaller the better)	1	tablespoon basil
¼	cup olive oil	1	teaspoon oregano
1	tablespoon minced garlic	½	teaspoon dried red pepper flakes
2	(26 ounce) cans Italian plum tomatoes	2	tablespoons capers
⅓	cup chopped fresh parsley	⅓	cup black olives
		8	ounces spaghetti

Wash clams well. Heat oil and garlic; cook about 30 seconds. Add tomatoes, parsley, basil, oregano, red pepper, capers and olives. Cook over medium-high heat for about 30 minutes, stirring frequently. Add the clams and cook, covered, for 5 minutes or until all the clams are open. Cook spaghetti according to package directions; drain and cover with clam sauce.

 This is great even without the clams.

Yield: 6 servings

WHITE CLAM SPAGHETTI

4	(6½ ounce) cans baby clams		Salt and pepper to taste
1	cup butter	2	tablespoons cornstarch
6	garlic cloves, minced	½	pint whipping cream
1	tablespoon lemon juice	½	cup fresh chopped parsley
1	tablespoon grated onion	8	ounces spaghetti

Drain clams and reserve juice. In heavy skillet, mix juice of clams, butter, garlic, lemon juice, onion, salt and pepper. Cook about 15 minutes. Dissolve cornstarch in cream and add to mixture along with clams and parsley; cook until thickened. Cook noodles according to package directions; drain, cover with sauce and serve.

Yield: 4 to 6 servings

CRAB CANNELLONI

15	Cannelloni	1	cup grated Parmesan
¾	cup plus 1 tablespoon		cheese
	butter	3	tablespoons tomato paste
½	cup flour	½	teaspoon salt
5	cups warm milk	½	teaspoon ground pepper
1	teaspoon nutmeg	1	pound fresh mushrooms
3	cups fresh crabmeat	1	tablespoon dried sage
2	egg yolks	3	tablespoons butter
1	pound mozzarella cheese,		
	cubed		

Preheat oven to 400°. Cook cannelloni according to package directions; drain and toss with 1 tablespoon butter. Melt ¾ cup butter in pan; add flour and stir to smooth paste. Gradually add milk and stir until thick. Add nutmeg. Remove half the sauce; set aside. Add crab and egg yolks to remaining sauce; add mozzarella cheese, salt and pepper. Stuff noodles with crab mixture; place in large, greased baking dish. Add tomato paste and ½ cup Parmesan cheese to reserved white sauce and spoon over noodles. Sauté mushrooms in sage and butter; arrange on top of casserole and sprinkle with remaining Parmesan cheese and a few dots of butter. Bake for 25 to 30 minutes.

   Chicken may be substituted for crabmeat.

Yield: 6 servings

ANGEL HAIR PASTA WITH CRAB

1½	cups butter	4	teaspoons chopped fresh
4	teaspoons chopped		parsley
	shallots	6	cups peeled, chopped
4	teaspoons chopped fresh		tomatoes
	basil	1	pound backfin crabmeat
		20	ounces angel hair pasta

Melt butter in saucepan. Add shallots, basil, parsley and tomatoes. Bring to a boil; add crabmeat. Cook pasta according to package directions; drain and cover with sauce.

Yield: 4 servings

FETTUCCINE WITH SMOKED SALMON

8	ounces fettuccine	½	cup sour cream
½	cup half-and-half cream	¼	pound smoked salmon
1	garlic clove, minced	½	cup grated Parmesan
1	teaspoon chopped dill		cheese
1	teaspoon prepared mustard		

Cook fettuccine according to package directions; set aside. Heat cream, garlic, dill and mustard in small saucepan. Stir in sour cream. Cut salmon into small pieces and add to sauce. Place fettuccine in warm serving dish and top with sauce and cheese.

Yield: 2 servings

GABLE SCALLOPS WITH PASTA

1	pound scallops	1	(10½ ounce) can Cheddar cheese soup
	Flour		
½	cup olive oil	⅓	cup milk
	Minced garlic		Fresh minced parsley
	Minced shallots		Oregano
3	large fresh tomatoes		Salt and pepper to taste
1	(10½ ounce) can cream of mushroom soup	8	ounces cooked spinach noodles

Flour scallops; brown in olive oil with garlic and shallots. Add peeled and chopped tomatoes; stir until blended. Combine soups with milk; add browned scallop mixture, parsley, oregano, salt and pepper. Stir in noodles until well blended. Heat until hot, but do not boil.

Yield: 4 to 6 servings

SHRIMP ALFREDO WITH ANGEL HAIR PASTA

16	ounces angel hair pasta	2	(10½ ounce) cans chicken broth
1½	pounds shrimp		
1	tablespoon chopped scallions	4-5	tablespoons prepared Alfredo sauce
1	tablespoon butter	3	tablespoons cream cheese
1	cup sliced shiitake mushrooms		Salt and pepper to taste
		1	tablespoon sherry
			Chopped parsley

Cook pasta according to package directions; drain and keep warm. Peel and clean shrimp; sauté in butter with scallions. Place in bowl; set aside. Sauté mushrooms until tender; set aside with shrimp. Pour chicken broth into pan and cook down by two-thirds. Add Alfredo sauce and cream cheese. Blend until smooth. Add shrimp and mushrooms; season with salt, pepper and sherry. Pour over pasta, garnish with parsley, and serve.

Yield: 4 to 6 servings

SHRIMP FETTUCCINE ALFREDO

1	pound shrimp	1	cup whipping cream
16	ounces fettuccine	1	egg, beaten
1	garlic clove, chopped		Salt and pepper to taste
½	cup butter	½	cup chopped parsley
1	cup grated Parmesan cheese		

Peel, clean and cook shrimp; set aside. Cook fettuccine according to package directions; drain and keep warm. Sauté garlic in melted butter; add grated cheese and cream. When cheese is melted, add egg, salt and pepper. Mix in shrimp and toss with fettuccine. Sprinkle parsley on top and serve.

Yield: 6 servings

VERMICELLI SHRIMP WITH FETA

1	pound medium shrimp	1	(28 ounce) can Italian
	Pinch of crushed red		plum tomatoes,
	pepper flakes		undrained
4	tablespoons olive oil,	¼	cup dry white wine
	divided	¾	teaspoon dried basil
4	ounces crumbled feta	½	teaspoon oregano
	cheese	¼	teaspoon salt
2	garlic cloves, minced	¼	teaspoon pepper
		8	ounces vermicelli

Preheat oven to 400°. Sauté shrimp and red pepper flakes in 2 tablespoons olive oil for 1 to 2 minutes. Peel and clean shrimp and arrange in casserole; sprinkle with cheese and set aside. Add remaining oil in skillet and sauté garlic over low heat. Add tomatoes and cook 1 minute. Stir in wine, basil, oregano, salt, pepper and simmer, uncovered, for 10 minutes. Pour tomato mixture over shrimp. Bake for 10 to 15 minutes or until bubbly. Cook vermicelli according to package directions; drain, cover with sauce and serve.

Yield: 4 servings

SHRIMP TETRAZZINI

1½	cups shrimp	1	(10½ ounce) can cream of
1¼	cups thin spaghetti		mushroom soup
¼	cup finely chopped green	1½	cups grated sharp
	pepper		Cheddar cheese
¼	cup finely chopped onion	¼	teaspoon salt
1	(4 ounce) jar pimientos	¼	teaspoon pepper

Preheat oven to 350°. Clean, cook, drain and cut up shrimp. Break spaghetti into small pieces; cook and drain. Mix remaining ingredients, reserving ¼ cup cheese for top. Pour into buttered casserole, top with cheese, and bake for 25 to 30 minutes, just until cheese melts.

Yield: 4 servings

LINGUINE WITH SHRIMP AND SCALLOPS

8	ounces linguine	1	cup tomato sauce
1	cup chopped watercress	½	cup half-and-half cream
	leaves	½	teaspoon mace
1	red pepper, finely	½	teaspoon black pepper
	chopped	1	pound shrimp, peeled and
2	garlic cloves, minced		deveined
2	tablespoons olive oil	½	pound scallops
½	cup white wine		

Cook linguine according to package directions; drain and keep warm. Sauté watercress, red pepper and garlic in olive oil for 3 minutes over low heat. Add wine and boil for 1 minute. Add tomato sauce and simmer for 10 minutes. Stir in cream, mace and pepper. Heat thoroughly. Add raw shrimp and scallops and cook for 5 minutes. Place linguine in serving bowl and top with sauce.

Yield: 4 to 6 servings

TORTELLINI WITH BASIL CREAM SAUCE

8	ounces tortellini	½	teaspoon white pepper
1	cup firmly packed fresh	1	cup half-and-half cream
	basil leaves	½	cup whipping cream
¼	cup olive oil	1	cup grated Romano
1	tablespoon pine nuts		cheese
2	garlic cloves		

While cooking tortellini according to package directions, combine next 5 ingredients in processor. Simmer creams and whisk in basil mixture and cheese. Heat and toss with warm pasta.

Yield: 4 servings

SEAFOOD LINGUINE

16	ounces linguine	¼	teaspoon basil
½	pound medium shrimp	1	(28 ounce) can crushed
4	garlic cloves, minced		tomatoes
3	tablespoons oil	½	pound small bay scallops
1	cup dry white wine		Grated Romano cheese
¼	teaspoon oregano		

Cook linguine according to package directions; drain and keep warm. Peel and devein shrimp. Sauté garlic in oil, being careful not to burn. Add wine and simmer for 5 minutes. Add oregano, basil and tomatoes and simmer for 1 hour or until sauce thickens. Add shrimp and scallops last 5 minutes of simmer. Pour over linguine and toss. Serve with Romano cheese.

Yield: 4 to 6 servings

BOOTH HOUSE

The Booth House, built circa 1779, offers a visit into one of Edenton's oldest dwellings. The distinctive gambrel roof house was built in two stages during the late eighteenth century. Its character reveals a history of various owners, who made interesting changes and additions to the original structure. The home encourages a relaxing pause on the porch or in the pleasant garden.

Entrées

ENTREES

BEEF EN GELÉE

1	5 to 7 pound beef tenderloin, trimmed	½	cup dry white wine
½	teaspoon salt	2	carrots
½	teaspoon ground pepper	1	cup sliced mushrooms
2	envelopes unflavored gelatin	2	cups cauliflower florets
		2	cups whole green beans
3	(10½ ounce) cans beef consommé	8-10	cherry tomatoes
		2	cups Italian dressing
			Parsley sprigs to garnish

Preheat oven to 425°. Rub beef with salt and pepper. Bake until meat thermometer reads 140°-160° (rare to medium). Cover and refrigerate overnight. Soak gelatin in consommé; heat until dissolved, stirring constantly. Remove from stove and add wine. Divide the mixture into 3 parts. Layer first third of gelatin into a serving platter; refrigerate until set. Cook carrots until slightly tender and slice. Arrange carrot and mushroom slices on gelatin layer and cover with another layer of consommé mixture; chill until set. Slice beef in ¼-inch slices and place in center of platter on gelatin, keeping the shape of the tenderloin. Spoon remaining gelatin mixture over beef to form a glaze. Chill thoroughly. Marinate cauliflower florets, beans and tomatoes for 3 or 4 hours in dressing. When ready to serve, drain vegetables and arrange around beef. Garnish with parsley.

 Read it again, it is not as difficult as it sounds! Can be made a day ahead.

Yield: 10 to 12 servings

FILET MIGNON WITH MUSTARD CREAM SAUCE

2	filet mignon steaks, 1¼ inches thick		Salt to taste
	Ground pepper	1	green onion, minced
1	tablespoon butter, divided	1	tablespoon brandy
		⅓	cup whipping cream
½	tablespoon vegetable oil	½	teaspoon Dijon mustard
			Fresh parsley sprigs

Grind pepper generously over both sides of filets and press into meat. Melt ½ tablespoon butter with oil in skillet over high heat. Salt filets on 1 side and add to skillet, salted side down. Cook until brown, about 2 minutes. Salt tops, turn and cook until brown. Reduce heat to medium and cook to desired doneness, turning occasionally, about 6 minutes for rare. Transfer filets to heated plates; set aside. Sauté onions in remaining ½ tablespoon butter; remove from heat and add brandy. Return to heat and bring to a boil, scraping pan often. Boil until reduced to a glaze. Add cream and cook until mixture begins to thicken, about 1 minute. Stir in mustard and any juices from filet plate. Remove from heat; season with salt and pepper. Spoon sauce over filets and garnish with parsley.

Yield: 2 servings

UP COUNTY STEAK

2	pounds lean round steak	1	(14½ ounce) can tomato wedges
2	large garlic cloves, minced		
2	medium onions, sliced	1	tablespoon A-1 sauce
2	green peppers, sliced	1	package mushroom beef gravy mix
3	stalks celery, chopped with tops		
		1	package onion soup mix
		1	(6 ounce) can mushrooms

Preheat oven to 350°. Cut steak in strips. Mix all ingredients well and bake, covered, for 1 hour. Serve over rice or noodles.

 Can be made the night before and refrigerated until ready to cook.

Yield: 4 to 6 servings

FREEMASON FILET IN PASTRY

1	3 pound beef tenderloin		2	shallots, minced
	Salt		1	package phyllo pastry
2	tablespoons sweet butter		½	cup melted butter
½	pound minced mushrooms			

Madeira Sauce

3	tablespoons butter		1	teaspoon Kitchen
1½	tablespoons flour			Bouquet
1	cup beef broth		¼	cup Madeira wine

Preheat oven to 400°. Rub filet with salt. In heavy skillet, sear the meat over high heat in butter until brown on all sides to seal in juices; set aside. In same pan, sauté mushrooms and shallots for 2 to 3 minutes until soft; set aside. Layer 12 pieces of phyllo pastry together, brushing each layer with melted butter. Spread half the mushroom mixture on pastry and place beef on top. Place remaining mushrooms on beef and fold phyllo dough around beef. Prepare an additional 5 to 6 phyllo layers, brush each with butter. Seal all edges by overlapping them with the additional pastry and brush with butter. Place beef in a buttered pan and bake for 45 minutes or until pastry is brown and flaky. Remove to serving dish.

Melt butter, stir in flour, and cook for 2 minutes. Add broth, Kitchen Bouquet and wine. Cook until thickened. Add more broth if necessary. Serve with beef.

 Elegant and easy. May be made ahead, sliced and served cold for a buffet.

Yield: 4 to 6 servings

BEEF WESSINGTON

1	3 to 3½ pound beef tenderloin	¼	cup finely chopped black olives
1	(8 ounce) package liverwurst spread	1	(16 ounce) package frozen puff pastry
½	cup finely chopped mushrooms	6	bacon slices
			Salt and pepper to taste
2	tablespoons Cognac	1	egg
		1	tablespoon milk

Preheat oven to 425°. Lightly salt and pepper all sides of tenderloin. Place on rack in shallow roasting pan, securing small end underneath. Wrap bacon slices around tenderloin and tie with string. Roast 20 to 25 minutes. Remove from oven; remove bacon and reserve. Cool to room temperature. Mix liverwurst, mushrooms, Cognac and olives; set aside. Remove puff pastry from freezer and let reach room temperature, about 20 minutes. Crumble bacon; add to liverwurst mixture and blend well. Roll pastry on lightly floured surface to 18x14 inches. Spread one-third of liverwurst mixture over top of tenderloin. Place top side down in middle of pastry and spread remaining liverwurst mixture over sides of tenderloin. Draw the long sides up to overlap slightly on the bottom of the beef, at least ½ inch. Beat egg and milk together and brush over pastry to seal. Trim ends of pastry and make an envelope fold, brushing with egg wash to seal. Transfer the pastry-covered meat to a lightly greased 13x9x2-inch pan. Roll out pastry trimmings, cut into decorative shapes and arrange on top of pastry. Brush egg wash evenly over entire pastry. Bake, uncovered, at 400° for approximately 30 minutes or until pastry is brown. Let stand 10 minutes before carving with very sharp knife.

 This is a show stopper and not so difficult to prepare.

Yield: 6 servings

HARVEY'S NECK BEEF AND BROCCOLI

½	pound round steak	2	tablespoons soy sauce
1	small garlic clove, minced	1½	pounds broccoli, cut into
2	teaspoons sugar		florets
1	teaspoon salt	¾	cup water
2	tablespoons oil	2	tablespoons cornstarch
2-4	tablespoons sake or	½	cup cold water
	sherry		Hot cooked rice

Cut steak into 1-inch cubes and stir fry with garlic, sugar and salt in hot oil. Stir in sake and soy sauce; cover and cook 2 to 3 minutes. Remove meat; set aside. Add broccoli and water to wok or pan. Bring to boil, stir, then cover for 2 to 5 minutes. Add meat. Combine cornstarch with cold water; mix well and pour over meat. Cook and stir 2 to 3 minutes. Serve warm over rice.

Yield: 4 servings

BEEF SHORT RIBS

2-4	pounds beef short ribs	1	garlic clove, crushed
½	cup flour	1	teaspoon thyme
½	teaspoon ground pepper	1	tablespoon Dijon mustard
3	onions, sliced	1½	tablespoons red wine
1	(10½ ounce) can beef		vinegar
	broth		Chopped parsley
1	bay leaf		

Preheat oven to 350°. Place meat, flour and pepper in plastic bag and shake to coat. In casserole, place half the sliced onions and layer beef on top. Layer remaining onions over beef. Mix broth, bay leaf, garlic and thyme; pour over beef and onions. Bake, covered, for 3½ hours. Remove beef from oven; place on a platter. Boil sauce to thicken and add mustard and vinegar. Stir and serve gravy over beef.

Stewing beef or pot roast may be used. Carrots may be added in last hour of cooking.

Yield: 4 servings

BEEF BURGUNDY

5	medium onions		Marjoram and thyme to
3	tablespoons bacon		taste
	drippings	½	cup beef broth, bouillon
2	pounds cubed lean beef		or consommé
1½	tablespoons flour	1	cup burgundy wine
	Salt and ground pepper to	½	pound sliced mushrooms
	taste		

Fry onions in bacon drippings until brown; remove to separate dish. In same drippings, brown beef on all sides; sprinkle with flour and a generous pinch each of salt, pepper, marjoram and thyme. Add beef broth and burgundy. Stir mixture; cook very slowly for 3¼ hours. As liquid cooks away, add more broth and wine so beef is always covered. Add onions and mushrooms; cook for another hour. The sauce should be thick, dark brown, and the aroma will be heavenly. Transfer to a deep serving dish and serve with rice or noodles.

Yield: 4 to 6 servings

HICKS FIELD STEW

1½	pounds cubed beef	1	cup water
2	tablespoons flour	1	(16 ounce) can tomatoes
	Salt and pepper to taste	1	tablespoon parsley
¼	cup butter	2	stalks celery, chopped
1	medium onion, sliced	4	carrots, chopped
1	garlic clove, minced	1	teaspoon thyme
1	cup sliced mushrooms	1	bay leaf
1	cup dry red wine		

Dredge beef in flour, salt and pepper; brown in butter. Add remaining ingredients; simmer for 2½ hours until beef is tender. Serve over rice.

Potatoes are also good in this stew.

Make ahead for Friday night ball games. Freezes well.

Yield: 4 servings

COUNTRY CLUB GOLFER'S STEW

1½	pounds cubed beef	½	teaspoon salt
1	medium onion, diced	1	teaspoon sugar
4	carrots, sliced	1	tablespoon cornstarch
4	potatoes, sliced	1	(12 ounce) can V-8 juice
½	teaspoon lemon pepper		

Preheat oven to 250°. Put meat into greased casserole. Layer onions, carrots and potatoes on top. Add lemon pepper, salt, sugar and cornstarch. Cover with V-8 juice and bake, covered, for 4 hours.

 Cooks while the cook plays golf!

Yield: 4 servings

BEEF WITH EGGPLANT

2	eggplants	2	(8 ounce) cans mushrooms, stems and pieces
6	yellow squash		
	Salt and pepper to taste		
	Sugar to taste	2	(14½ ounce) cans tomato wedges, drained
3	medium onions		
1	tablespoon oil	1	tablespoon Worcestershire sauce
2	pounds extra lean ground beef		
		2	cups herb stuffing mix
		1	cup grated Parmesan cheese

Preheat oven to 350°. Peel and dice eggplants into ¾-inch pieces; scrape, slice and quarter the squash. Steam the eggplant and squash for about 5 minutes; drain well. Add salt, pepper and sugar to taste. Sauté onion in oil; add beef and brown. Add mushrooms and simmer 5 minutes. Add steamed vegetables, tomatoes and Worcestershire sauce. Divide stuffing mix into 2 buttered 7x11-inch casseroles; pour half the vegetable/meat mixture into each casserole. Top each with grated cheese and bake for 30 minutes.

Yield: 12 servings

CAJUN MEAT LOAF

Seasoning Mix

2	whole bay leaves	½	teaspoon white pepper
1	tablespoon salt	½	teaspoon ground cumin
1	teaspoon cayenne pepper	½	teaspoon ground nutmeg
1	teaspoon black pepper		

Meat Loaf

4	tablespoons butter	1	tablespoon
¾	cup finely chopped onions		Worcestershire sauce
½	cup finely chopped celery	½	cup evaporated milk
½	cup finely chopped bell pepper	½	cup ketchup
		1½	pounds ground chuck
¼	cup finely chopped onions	½	pound ground pork
		2	eggs, lightly beaten
2	teaspoons minced garlic	1	cup dry breadcrumbs

Combine the seasoning mix ingredients; set aside.

Preheat oven to 350°. Melt butter and add next 6 meat loaf ingredients; add seasoning mix and sauté until mixture makes a paste, about 5 minutes. Stir and scrape bottom of pan well. Stir in milk and ketchup and continue cooking for 2 minutes, stirring occasionally. Remove from heat and cool mixture to room temperature. Place beef and pork in an ungreased 13x9-inch baking dish. Add eggs, seasoning mixture (with bay leaves removed), and breadcrumbs. Mix by hand until thoroughly combined. Shape the mixture into a loaf and bake, uncovered, for 45 minutes until desired doneness.

 Even non-meat loaf lovers love this!

Yield: 6 servings

JAMESVILLE MEAT LOAF

Meat

3	pounds ground chuck	3	teaspoons salt
⅓	cup chopped onion	½	cup canned tomatoes,
2	eggs, beaten		drained

Sauce

2	(8 ounce) cans tomato sauce	2	tablespoons prepared mustard
½	cup water	2	teaspoons Worcestershire sauce
3	tablespoons vinegar		
3	tablespoons brown sugar		

Preheat oven to 350°. Mix beef, onion, eggs, salt and tomatoes; shape into a loaf and place in a casserole dish with cover.

Mix sauce ingredients and pour over meat loaf. Bake, covered, for 1 hour and 15 minutes.

Yield: 6 to 8 servings

MOCK PAN PIZZA

1	pound lean ground beef	1	(8 ounce) can tomato sauce
1½	teaspoons salt		
¼	teaspoon pepper	½	teaspoon dry mustard
2	teaspoons horseradish	2	tablespoons minced onion
1	teaspoon Worcestershire sauce	2	tablespoons parsley
½	teaspoon dried basil or 2 basil leaves	1	cup grated sharp Cheddar cheese
		1	cup grated mozzarella cheese

Preheat oven to 350°. Mix ground beef with salt and pepper. Add horseradish, Worcestershire sauce and basil. Press meat mixture on sides and bottom of a casserole dish or a 9-inch pie pan. Spread tomato sauce over meat mixture. Combine mustard, onion, parsley, and cheeses. Spread cheese mixture evenly on top of casserole and bake for 20 minutes. Do not overbake!

Yield: 4 servings

PIZZA BIANCA

	Vegetable oil	2	tablespoons grated
1	uncooked pizza shell or		Parmesan cheese
	your favorite pizza dough	4	bacon slices, cooked and
8	ounces thin sliced		diced
	mozzarella		Ground pepper to taste
8	ounces drained ricotta	1-2	sprigs fresh rosemary
2	tablespoons shredded	8	fresh basil leaves
	provolone cheese	1	tablespoon olive oil

Preheat oven to 375°. Lightly coat a round pizza pan with vegetable oil. Press the dough into the pan. Layer all ingredients on top of dough in order they are listed. Bake for 10 to 15 minutes.

Yield: 1 pizza

HISTORIC HAMBURGER

1½	pounds lean ground beef	1	cup sour cream
2	tablespoons butter	6	green onions, chopped
	Salt and pepper to taste	12	ounces noodles, cooked
1	teaspoon sugar		and drained
1	garlic clove, minced	1	cup grated sharp Cheddar
2	cups tomato sauce		cheese
3	ounces cream cheese		

Preheat oven to 350°. Brown beef in butter; add salt, pepper, sugar, garlic and tomato sauce. Simmer for 20 minutes. Mix cream cheese, sour cream and green onions. Put layer of noodles, thin layer of cheese mixture, and layer of beef mixture in a casserole. Repeat layers. Grate Cheddar cheese over the top. Bake for 20 to 30 minutes.

Yield: 8 servings

LOCUST GROVE LAYERS

1	pound ground beef	2	zucchini or yellow
3	carrots, sliced		squash, sliced
3	stalks celery, sliced		Salt and pepper to taste
1-2	baking potatoes, peeled	1	teaspoon basil
	and sliced	1	teaspoon parsley
1	medium onion, sliced	¼	teaspoon tarragon
1	green pepper, chopped	1	(10½ ounce) can tomato
1	(4 ounce) can mushrooms,		soup
	drained		

Preheat oven to 350°. Layer uncooked beef, carrots, celery, potatoes, onion, pepper, mushrooms and squash in a 2-quart casserole. Cover with spices and soup and bake, uncovered, for 2 hours. Serve with French bread and a tossed salad.

Tarragon is the secret ingredient. Children love this!

Yield: 6 servings

COURTHOUSE CASSEROLE

2	pounds lean ground beef	8	ounces sour cream
2	tablespoons oil	3	ounces cream cheese
1	teaspoon salt	8	ounces noodles, cooked
1	onion, finely chopped		and drained
2	(8 ounce) jars spaghetti	1	cup grated Cheddar
	sauce with mushrooms		cheese
8	ounces cottage cheese		

Preheat oven to 350°. Brown beef in oil; add salt, onion and spaghetti sauce and simmer for 20 minutes. For cheese mixture, mix together cottage cheese, sour cream and cream cheese. In buttered casserole, put layer of noodles, layer of meat and layer of cheese mixture. Repeat layer of noodles and layer of meat. Top with Cheddar cheese and bake for 35 minutes.

Good for a crowd! Can be made ahead and frozen.

Yield: 8 servings

SATTERFIELD STIR-FRY BEEF

1½	pounds top round steak	1	(8 ounce) can tomato
¼	cup corn oil		sauce
1	small onion, sliced	1	teaspoon sugar
1½	cups sliced celery	½	teaspoon ground ginger
¾	cup thinly sliced carrots	1	small green pepper
1	tablespoon cornstarch	½	cup mushrooms
¼	cup soy sauce	3	cups cooked rice

Trim steak and cut into thin, 2-inch strips. Sear in oil. Separate onion slices into rings and add to skillet with celery and carrots. Stir-fry until crisp tender. Blend cornstarch with soy sauce in small bowl and stir in tomato sauce and seasonings. Cut green pepper into strips and add to skillet with mushrooms. Stir-fry about 5 minutes longer until sauce thickens and becomes shiny. Serve over rice.

Yield: 4 to 6 servings

CORNERSTONE CURRIED LAMB

1	large onion, chopped	1	(10½ ounce) can beef or
2	garlic cloves, minced		chicken broth
3	tablespoons melted butter	1	red apple, cored and diced
1	tablespoon curry powder	2-3	cups leftover cooked lamb
3	tablespoons flour		Hot cooked rice

Sauté onion and garlic in butter until soft. Stir in curry powder and flour; cook until bubbly. Gradually stir in broth and cook, stirring, until thickened. Add apple and lamb. Cover and simmer for 15 to 20 minutes. Serve over rice and pass condiments of your choice.

 Leftover beef or poultry can be used.

Yield: 4 to 6 servings

MEDALLIONS OF LAMB WITH ARTICHOKE AND TOMATO

2	cups cleaned and diced artichoke hearts	4	ounces sliced fois gras
¼	cup butter	¼	cup truffle juice
4	medium tomatoes, peeled, seeded and diced	2	lamb loins, boned and trimmed
1	cup whipping cream	¼	cup butter
	Salt and pepper to taste		Fresh basil leaves

Sauté artichokes for 2 minutes in butter. Add tomatoes and cook an additional 3 minutes. Pour in cream, very slowly. Simmer until thick and artichoke pieces are tender; add salt and pepper. Lightly fold in fois gras and add truffle juice. Season lamb with salt and pepper; sauté in butter in hot saucepan to medium rare. To serve, spoon artichoke sauce onto center of warm plates. Slice lamb into 10 medallions and place on top of sauce. Garnish with more sauce and fresh basil leaves.

Yield: 4 servings

LEG OF LAMB WITH HONEY MUSTARD SAUCE

1	3 pound leg of lamb	1	cup dry red wine
4	tablespoons finely chopped shallots	⅔	cup whipping cream
4	tablespoons butter, divided	1	teaspoon rosemary
			Salt and pepper to taste
⅔	cup sliced mushrooms	4	tablespoons honey mustard
2	garlic cloves, minced		

Preheat oven to 350°. Butterfly, roll and tie leg of lamb. Sauté shallots in 2 tablespoons butter until translucent; add mushrooms. As mushrooms produce liquid, raise heat and cook until most has evaporated. Set aside. Brown lamb well on all sides in 2 tablespoons butter. Add shallots, mushrooms, garlic, wine, rosemary, salt and pepper. Spread mustard over lamb; bring to a simmer. Bake, covered, for 1½ hours. Let lamb rest for 10 minutes and remove to a cutting board. On top of stove, reduce the cooking liquid until it is almost a glaze. Add cream and boil for 1 minute. Salt and pepper to taste. Carve lamb and arrange slices on a warm platter. Cover with sauce and serve.

Yield: 4 to 6 servings

MULBERRY HILL MOUSSAKA

1-2	pounds sliced eggplant		Salt and pepper to taste
1	cup chopped onions	1	cup spaghetti sauce
2	cups ground lamb	½	cup grated mozzarella
2	garlic cloves, minced		cheese
1	teaspoon thyme	½	cup grated Parmesan
1	teaspoon oregano		cheese

Preheat oven to 375°. Boil eggplant slices 4 minutes until barely tender. Drain and pat dry on paper towels. Oil a 9x12-inch baking dish and cover bottom with a layer of eggplant. Sauté onions in a little oil and brown ground lamb. Pour off grease and add garlic and herbs. Spread layer of lamb mixture over eggplant, then one-fourth of spaghetti sauce and one-third of cheeses. Spread another layer of eggplant, lamb, sauce and cheeses —keep layering, ending with sauce and cheese. Cover with oiled foil and bake for 25 to 35 minutes. Remove foil and cook another 15 minutes.

 This is very good served with a simple green salad.

Yield: 8 servings

PILGRIMAGE COUNTRY HAM

1	country ham	Water to cover
½-1	cup vinegar	

Remove ham hock; scrub ham thoroughly in hot water. Soak in cold water for 24 hours, changing water often. Place ham in roaster, fat side up. Fill roaster with very hot water to the brim and add vinegar; cover, and bake at 250° for 4 hours. Turn oven off and turn ham over, fat side down. Leave ham, covered, in closed oven for 45 minutes. Remove ham from stock and cool slightly before cutting off skin.

 Hams are cooked, using this method, for the St. Paul's Pilgrimage Luncheon.

CALVES LIVER IN WINE SAUCE

1	large onion, minced	¼	teaspoon paprika
8	tablespoons butter	2	pounds thin sliced calves
½	cup beef pan gravy		liver
¾	cup red wine	3	tablespoons apple brandy
½	teaspoon tarragon vinegar	½	teaspoon salt
½	teaspoon basil		

Sauté onion in 4 tablespoons butter until golden brown. Add beef gravy and wine; boil until one-half reduced. Add tarragon vinegar, basil and paprika; simmer 15 minutes to make sauce. Cut liver into 2½-inch squares. Sauté approximately 1 minute per side in remaining 4 tablespoons butter. Add brandy and salt. Pour sauce over liver and serve.

Yield: 4 servings

HORNIBLOW POINT PORK ROAST

1	3½ pound center cut pork roast, boned	2-3	tablespoons dried dill weed
1	garlic clove, minced	1	teaspoon black pepper
2	tablespoons garlic powder	½	teaspoon salt
2	tablespoons chopped parsley		

Preheat oven to 300°. Untie roast and score fat. Make random holes and insert minced garlic. Mix remaining spices and pat some into roast; re-tie. Spread remaining spice mixture on a 12-inch piece of waxed paper. Roll roast on paper to coat with spices. Place in roasting pan with ½ cup of water. Bake until desired doneness, about 1 to 1½ hours. Let stand to room temperature before carving.

 Makes wonderful sandwiches or is great on a buffet table, served with Dijon mustard.

Yield: 4 to 6 servings

MARINATED PORK TENDERLOINS

4	pork tenderloins	½	cup zesty Italian dressing
½	cup soy or teriyaki sauce		

Mix together sauce and dressing and marinate meat overnight. Grill outside or bake at 350° for 30 to 45 minutes.

 Slice and serve with honey mustard and sesame seeds as an hors d'oeuvre. Dip with toothpick first in mustard, then sesame seeds.

Yield: 8 to 10 servings

PORK CHOPS SAUTHIER

6	pork chops	¼	cup white wine
	Garlic salt and pepper	2-3	tablespoons whipping
2	tablespoons butter		cream
½	cup finely chopped onion	4	ounces grated mozzarella
½	cup sliced mushrooms		or Monterey Jack cheese
½	cup breadcrumbs		

Preheat oven to 350°. Salt and pepper both sides of chops and brown in butter. Place in single layer in casserole. Sauté onion and mushrooms; stir in breadcrumbs. Add wine and enough cream to make a light stuffing. Stir and mound over chops. Sprinkle each with grated cheese and bake for 40 to 45 minutes.

Yield: 6 servings

PORK CHOPS WITH BLACK CURRANT PRESERVES

4	boned pork chops, ¾-inch thick	1½	tablespoons Dijon mustard
¼	cup black currant preserves	¼	cup white wine vinegar
			Salt and pepper

Brown chops in salted skillet. Mix preserves and mustard and spread over chops. Reduce heat, cover, and simmer for 30 minutes. Remove chops from pan and add vinegar to sauce and drippings; reduce sauce and pour over chops.

Yield: 2 to 4 servings

SWEET AND SOUR PORK CHOPS

Pork Chops

6	pork chops, 1 inch thick	Flour for dredging
	Salt and pepper to taste	Water

Sauce

½	cup vinegar	1	tablespoon
2	tablespoons melted butter		Worcestershire sauce
½	cup water	1	tablespoon flour
1	teaspoon mustard	½	teaspoon Tabasco
3	tablespoons brown sugar	2	tablespoons ketchup

Preheat oven to 350°. Salt, pepper and flour chops. Place in buttered casserole; cover with water and cook for 30 to 45 minutes. Mix sauce ingredients; pour over chops and bake for 1 hour.

 A rice dish makes a nice accompaniment.

Yield: 6 servings

PEMBROKE PLANTATION PORK CHOPS

6	pork chops	½	cup diced celery
	Salt and pepper		Dash of Tabasco sauce
2	teaspoons olive oil	6	onion rings
6	beef bouillon cubes	6	green pepper slices
2½	cups boiling water	6	tomato slices
1	cup uncooked rice		

Preheat oven to 325°. Salt, pepper and brown pork chops in oil. Dissolve bouillon cubes in boiling water. Add rice, celery and Tabasco; mix well. Pour into casserole and place chops on rice. Top each chop with onion ring, green pepper and tomato. Bake, covered, for 45 minutes.

Yield: 6 servings

PAMLICO PORK

1	4 pound pork loin		Ground pepper to taste
16	pitted prunes	1	teaspoon ground ginger
¼	cup butter	½	teaspoon paprika
½	lemon, juiced		

Preheat oven to 350°. Push skewer through length of loin. With handle of a wooden spoon, make a large hole in pork loin. Push prunes one by one to fill cavity, making sure prunes reach entire length of loin. Melt butter; add juice of lemon, pepper, ginger and paprika. Pour over loin and bake, covered, for 30 minutes. Roast, uncovered, an additional 1 hour and 20 minutes, basting every half hour.

 Elegant, the prunes make it!

Yield: 8 servings

STUFFED PORK CHOPS IN WINE

8	pork chops, thinly sliced	½	cup seedless raisins
	Salt and pepper	1	cup chopped apple
½	cup finely chopped celery	1	cup soft breadcrumbs
½	cup finely chopped green pepper	½	teaspoon salt
		⅛	teaspoon pepper
¼	cup finely chopped onion	¾	cup dry white wine

Preheat oven to 350°. Cut any excess fat from chops and sprinkle both sides with salt and pepper. Brown chops, on one side only, in hot fat. (Fat from chops can be used). Combine celery, pepper, onion, raisins, apple, breadcrumbs, salt and pepper; mix well. Place 4 chops in a casserole, browned side down, and top with mixture. Cover with remaining chops, browned side up. Skewer with picks and sprinkle with wine. Bake, covered, for 1 hour or until very tender.

Yield: 4 servings

BOURBON SPARERIBS

12	pounds country style spareribs	1	cup Dijon mustard
1	cup brown sugar	2½	tablespoons Worcestershire sauce
½	cup soy sauce	¼	cup finely chopped onion
¼	cup orange juice	½	cup bourbon

Separate ribs with knife; arrange in 13x9-inch dish. In separate bowl, blend brown sugar, soy sauce and orange juice; add mustard, Worcestershire sauce, onion and bourbon. Pour 3 cups of marinade over ribs, saving 1 cup for basting. Cover dish tightly and marinate overnight. Preheat oven to 350° and bake on rack in roasting pan for 1½ to 2 hours. Baste with marinade every 25 minutes. Place under broiler last 8 to 10 minutes to crisp ribs, basting twice.

   Tender and delicious!

Yield: 10 to 12 servings

DURANT'S NECK APPLES AND SAUSAGE

1	cup uncooked rice		Brown sugar
	Salt	2	cups water
1	package link sausage	¼	cup ketchup
2	large tart apples		

Preheat oven to 350°. Cook rice in boiling, salted water until done. Cover sausage with some of the boiling water and let stand for 3 minutes; drain on towel. Core and slice apples; place in bottom of 2-quart casserole, sprinkle with brown sugar. Drain rice and spread over apples. Layer sausage on rice; cover with ketchup and bake, covered, for 45 minutes. Uncover and bake an additional 15 minutes.

   Granny Smith apples are best.

Yield: 4 to 6 servings

PETTIGREW SAUSAGE-RICE

1	pound sausage	1	cup diced carrots
1	cup uncooked rice	1-2	tablespoons butter
1	small onion, diced	2	cups chicken broth
1	cup diced celery		

Preheat oven to 350°. Cook, drain, and crumble sausage. Put rice in the bottom of a greased, 3-quart casserole. Sauté onion, celery and carrots in butter. Combine with cooked sausage and place on top of rice. Cover with broth. Cover tightly with foil and bake for 30 minutes. Stir and cook for an additional 30 minutes.

Yield: 6 to 8 servings

MERRY HILL VEAL MARSALA

8	veal slices	2	tablespoons chopped parsley
	Flour to dredge		
2	tablespoons butter	1	tablespoon flour
1	tablespoon olive oil		Salt and pepper to taste
	Paprika	1	(10½ ounce) can beef bouillon
½	pound mushrooms		
2	tablespoons chopped chives	½	cup Marsala wine

Preheat oven to 350°. Pound veal into cutlets and flour. Sauté on both sides in butter and oil and transfer to casserole in single layer; sprinkle with paprika. Wipe out sauté pan and add butter; sauté mushrooms, chives, parsley, salt and pepper. Add 1 tablespoon flour; stir until cooked. Add broth and wine; simmer 5 minutes. Pour sauce over veal. Bake, covered, for 30 minutes.

 The gravy this dish makes is fantastic over mashed potatoes.

Yield: 8 servings

VEAL SCALLOPINI MARSALA

1½	pounds of veal scallops	½	cup Marsala wine
	Flour	½	cup sliced mushrooms
½	teaspoon ground oregano		Salt to taste
	Butter		

Pound veal very thin and dust with flour and oregano. Quickly brown each scallop in butter and transfer to a platter. Add wine and mushrooms into pan drippings; scrape and deglaze pan. Return veal to pan; simmer until veal is tender. Salt to taste. Serve with rice.

 For special occasions, add ¼ cup whipping cream.

Yield: 2 to 4 servings

VEAL WITH OLIVES AND CAPERS

2	tablespoons olive oil	1	tablespoon butter
¼	cup flour	½	cup dry white wine
1½	pounds veal cutlets	8	olives, thinly sliced
	Ground pepper to taste	1	tablespoon capers

Heat oil over high heat. Lightly flour veal and sauté until golden, about 2 to 3 minutes a side. Transfer cutlets to a heated platter and sprinkle with pepper. Melt butter over high heat in same skillet; add wine, stirring rapidly and scraping up browned bits. Reduce heat; add olives and capers. Cook for 1 to 2 minutes; pour sauce over veal and serve.

Yield: 3 to 4 servings

PEACH SALSA FOR HAMBURGERS

1	peach	½	teaspoon sugar
1	tomato	1	teaspoon Balsamic
1	garlic clove		vinegar
	Jalapeño pepper to taste		Salt and pepper to taste

Coarsely chop peach and tomato; mince garlic clove. Mix all ingredients together while hamburgers are on the grill and buns are warming. Serve salsa over hot burgers!

Yield: Sauce for 4 to 6 burgers

GRILLED MEAT MARINADE

1	large garlic clove	½	teaspoon Dijon mustard
1½	tablespoons blue cheese	2	teaspoons instant coffee
1	teaspoon salt	2	tablespoons dry vermouth
1	teaspoon pepper	½	cup olive oil

Crush garlic and crumble blue cheese; add remaining ingredients and mix well. Marinate meat at room temperature for 3 hours, turning occasionally. Grill, slice, and serve.

To serve cold, wrap in aluminum foil and refrigerate. Slice when ready to serve.

Recipe calls for sirloin steak, however, eye of the round and other cuts work nicely as well.

Yield: ¾ cup marinade

MARINADE FOR FLANK STEAK OR CHICKEN

1	(16 ounce) jar Kraft Italian dressing	½	cup soy sauce
		1	teaspoon ginger
½	cup honey	3	teaspoons minced garlic

Mix all ingredients well and marinate steak or chicken all day or overnight.

Yield: 2 cups marinade

BANDON CHAPEL CHICKEN BREASTS

6	chicken breasts, skinned	⅓	cup white wine
6	slices of cheese (your preference)	1	(8 ounce) package herb dressing mix
1	(10½ ounce) can cream of celery or cream of chicken soup	¼	cup melted butter

Preheat oven to 350°. Lay chicken breasts in baking dish; top each with a slice of cheese. Mix soup with wine; pour over chicken. Cover with dressing mix; drizzle with melted butter and bake for 45 minutes.

Yield: 6 servings

RIVER CHICKEN KIEV

4	whole chicken breasts	4	tablespoons softened
½	cup fine dry breadcrumbs		butter
½	cup grated Parmesan	1	tablespoon chopped
	cheese		parsley
1½	teaspoons oregano	4	ounces Monterey Jack
½	teaspoon garlic salt		cheese
¼	teaspoon pepper	5	tablespoons melted butter

Bone, split and skin chicken breasts. Gently pound between sheets of wax paper until ¼ inch thick; set aside. Combine breadcrumbs, Parmesan cheese, 1 teaspoon of oregano, garlic salt and pepper; set aside. Stir together 4 tablespoons butter, parsley and remaining oregano; set aside. Cut cheese into 8 strips, ½ inch thick and 1½ inches long; set aside. Spread ½ tablespoon of herb/butter mixture across each breast; lay strip of cheese on top. Fold and enclose filling. Dip each bundle in melted butter; roll in breadcrumb mixture. Place, seam side down, in baking pan; drizzle with remaining butter. Cover and refrigerate for at least 4 hours. Preheat oven to 425° and bake for 20 minutes.

Yield: 6 to 8 servings

BLACK OLIVE CHICKEN

8	bacon slices	½	cup white wine
1-2	tablespoons flour	1	(2 ounce) jar pimientos,
8	chicken breasts, boned		drained
2-3	cups chicken bouillon	1	(8 ounce) jar mushrooms,
1	(6 ounce) can black		drained
	olives		

Preheat oven to 325°. Cook, drain and crumble bacon. Flour chicken and brown in bacon drippings. Remove chicken to flat baking dish. Add bouillon to pan scrapings and heat. Combine some of bouillon and flour in a small jar to blend. Pour back into pan and boil 2 minutes. Add bacon, olives, wine, pimientos and mushrooms to sauce until creamy; pour over chicken. Bake, uncovered, for 1 hour, basting occasionally.

Yield: 6 to 8 servings

CHAMBERS FERRY CHICKEN

2½	cups blanched broccoli florets	4	medium potatoes, cooked and mashed
2	cups grated Cheddar cheese, divided	2	(10½ ounce) cans cream of mushroom soup
4	chicken breasts, boned and skinned		

Preheat oven to 350°. In baking dish layer: broccoli, cheese, chicken and mashed potatoes; top with soup. Repeat layers, ending with soup. Sprinkle with grated cheese. Bake for 45 minutes until chicken is tender and sauce is bubbly.

Yield: 4 servings

CHICKEN BREAST WELLINGTON

1	package frozen puff pastry sheets		Salt and pepper to taste
1	(6 ounce) box wild rice mix	1	egg white
1	orange peel, grated	1	(12 ounce) jar red currant jelly
8	breast halves, boned and skinned	½	teaspoon Dijon mustard
		1	tablespoon orange juice
		2	tablespoons white wine

Thaw pastry according to directions. Cook rice mix according to package directions. Add orange peel. Pound chicken to flatten slightly; salt and pepper. Beat egg white until soft peaks form. Fold into rice. Cut pastry sheets into quarters; roll out to 8-inch squares. Place chicken in center with ⅓ cup rice on top. Roll chicken inside pastry, jelly roll fashion, turning edges in. Place, seam side down, on cookie sheet; refrigerate overnight. When ready to bake, preheat oven to 375° and bake, uncovered, 35 to 45 minutes. Combine remaining ingredients and heat. Serve warm over chicken.

Yield: 8 servings

CHICKEN BREASTS ROMANO

⅓	cup flour	½	teaspoon garlic salt
½	teaspoon salt	½	teaspoon oregano
¼	teaspoon pepper	½	teaspoon basil
6	chicken breasts	1	teaspoon vinegar
2	tablespoons vegetable oil	2	cups sliced mushrooms
¼	cup minced onion	1	teaspoon minced parsley
2	cups tomato juice	½	cup grated Parmesan
2	tablespoons grated		cheese
	Parmesan cheese	8	ounces hot, cooked
1	tablespoon sugar		spaghetti

Combine flour, salt and pepper. Dredge chicken in flour mixture and brown in hot oil. Drain on paper towels. Pour off all but 1 tablespoon of pan drippings. Sauté onion in drippings until tender. Add tomato juice, 2 tablespoons cheese, sugar, garlic salt, oregano, basil, vinegar, mushrooms and parsley. Return chicken to skillet; cover and simmer 45 minutes. At serving time, sprinkle chicken with ½ cup Parmesan cheese and serve over hot spaghetti.

Yield: 6 servings

MARINA CHICKEN DIVAN

4	cups broccoli florets	½	cup mayonnaise
6	chicken breasts, cooked	2	tablespoons lemon juice
	and boned		Curry powder to taste
1	(10½ ounce) can cream of		Grated Cheddar cheese
	chicken soup		Breadcrumbs (optional)
1	(10½ ounce) can cream of		Parsley
	celery soup		

Preheat oven to 350°. Slightly cook broccoli and put in bottom of 2-quart casserole dish. Place chicken breasts (in big chunks) on top of broccoli. Mix next 5 ingredients; spread over chicken and broccoli. Grate cheese on top and sprinkle with breadcrumbs and parsley. Bake for 40 minutes or until bubbly.

Yield: 8 servings

CHICKEN WITH MUSHROOM SAUCE

6	chicken breasts, boned and skinned	1	tablespoon cornstarch
¼	cup butter	½	teaspoon pepper
1	(14 ounce) can artichoke hearts, drained	1	teaspoon paprika
		1	teaspoon chicken flavored bouillon
1½	cups sliced mushrooms	⅔	cup water
3	tablespoons thinly sliced green onions	¼	cup dry sherry
		½	teaspoon dried rosemary
4	garlic cloves, minced		

Preheat oven to 375°. Brown both sides of chicken in butter. Remove chicken from pan and sauté artichoke hearts, mushrooms, onions and garlic. Combine cornstarch and remaining ingredients; pour into skillet and bring to a boil. Boil 1 minute, stirring constantly. Place chicken in greased baking dish and cover with sauce. Bake, covered, for 30 to 40 minutes.

Yield: 6 servings

PLUMB WALK CHICKEN SUPREME

4	chicken breasts, halved, boned and skinned	¼	cup white wine or sherry
		½	teaspoon rosemary
8	bacon slices		Salt and pepper to taste
½	cup cooked and cubed country ham	1	garlic clove, minced
		1	teaspoon paprika
1	(10½ ounce) can cream of mushroom soup	½	cup grated Swiss or Parmesan cheese
1	cup sour cream		

Wrap chicken breasts in bacon slices. Sprinkle ham on bottom of 9x13-inch buttered baking dish; place wrapped breasts on top. Combine mushroom soup, sour cream, wine, rosemary, salt, pepper, garlic and paprika. Mix well and pour over chicken. Cover and chill overnight or for several hours. When ready to serve, preheat oven to 350° and bake for 50 minutes. Sprinkle with cheese and continue baking until cheese melts, about 10 minutes.

Yield: 8 servings

CHICKEN TETRAZZINI

16	ounces spaghetti	1	(10½ ounce) can cream of
8	chicken breasts, cooked		mushroom soup
	and cubed	1	(10½ ounce) can cream of
1	small onion, chopped		chicken soup
1	green pepper, chopped	1	(10½ ounce) can chicken
1	(4 ounce) can chopped		broth
	pimiento	8	ounces grated sharp
⅛	teaspoon red pepper		Cheddar cheese
		½	cup slivered almonds

Preheat oven to 350°. Cook spaghetti according to package directions; drain. Combine all ingredients except cheese and almonds. Blend well, adding chicken broth as needed to bring to consistency of medium cream sauce. Pour into baking dish and top with cheese and almonds. Bake for 30 minutes.

  May be divided into desired servings and frozen.

Yield: 8 to 10 servings

CONFEDERATE CHICKEN

6	chicken breasts	1	cup whipping cream or
	Garlic salt to taste		half-and-half cream
	Paprika to taste		Chopped parsley to taste
1	(10½ ounce) can cream of		
	mushroom soup		

Preheat oven to 350°. Sprinkle chicken thoroughly on both sides with garlic salt and paprika. Lay chicken in casserole. Mix soup and cream together and pour over chicken. Sprinkle with lots of fresh parsley and bake, uncovered, for 1 to 1½ hours.

  The soup and cream mixture is wonderful over rice.

Yield: 4-6 servings

MARKETPLACE CHICKEN MADEIRA

12	chicken breasts, boned and skinned	1	tablespoon lemon juice
¾	cup flour	¼	cup water
1	teaspoon salt	2	garlic cloves, minced
¾	teaspoon pepper	3	tablespoons butter
¼	cup butter	1	pound sliced mushrooms
½	cup Madeira wine		Parsley

Preheat oven to 350°. Cover chicken breasts with wax paper and pound to ⅛-inch thick. Mix flour, salt and pepper and dredge chicken in mixture. Melt butter over moderate heat; cook chicken 2 to 3 minutes on each side until lightly browned, adding more butter as needed. Remove from pan and arrange in 9x13-inch baking dish; discard fat. Add wine, lemon juice and water; cook and stir, scraping pan to loosen brown bits. Add garlic; cook until liquid is boiling and syrupy. Pour over chicken; add butter to skillet and sauté mushrooms. Spoon over chicken; cover with foil and bake for 40 minutes until very hot. Garnish with parsley.

 May be refrigerated for 24 hours before baking.

Yield: 12 servings

FIERY CHICKEN

8	small chicken breasts	½	teaspoon ground cumin
2	tablespoons oil	¼	teaspoon cayenne pepper
1	medium onion, chopped	¼	teaspoon oregano
¼	cup soy sauce	1	cup water
2	garlic cloves, chopped	¼	cup water
2	teaspoons paprika	4	tablespoons cornstarch

Brown chicken breasts in hot oil; remove and set aside. Sauté onion in same pan. Add soy sauce, garlic, paprika, cumin, pepper, oregano and 1 cup of water; stir until blended. Return chicken and simmer for 25 minutes. Turn chicken and simmer 20 minutes more. Remove chicken; thicken pan juices with ¼ cup of water mixed with cornstarch. Serve chicken and gravy over rice or noodles.

Yield: 8 servings

LIGHTHOUSE LEMON CHICKEN

Sauce

1	tablespoon soy sauce	½	cup fresh lemon juice
½	teaspoon salt	2	tablespoons grated lemon
½	teaspoon pepper		peel
¼	cup vegetable oil	1	garlic clove, crushed

Chicken

½	cup flour	2	teaspoons paprika
½	teaspoon salt	8	chicken breasts
¼	teaspoon pepper	½	cup butter

Combine sauce ingredients at least 1 hour before cooking.

Preheat oven to 400°. Combine dry ingredients and coat chicken. Melt butter in baking dish and arrange chicken, skin side down, in a single layer. Cover with sauce; bake, uncovered, for 30 minutes. Turn chicken and cook an additional 30 minutes. Do not over cook!

Yield: 8 servings

MEXICAN CHICKEN

1	package crumbled tortilla chips	½	cup chopped onion
3-4	chicken breasts, cooked and chopped	½	cup chopped green pepper
1	(10½ ounce) can cream of mushroom soup	1	tablespoon garlic powder
1	(10½ ounce) can cream of chicken soup	1	tablespoon chili powder
1½	cups chicken broth	1	cup grated Cheddar cheese
1	(10 ounce) can Ro-Tel tomato and green chilies	½	cup grated Monterey Jack cheese

Preheat oven to 350°. Place a layer of tortilla chips in bottom of buttered 9x13-inch baking dish. Mix remaining ingredients, except Monterey Jack cheese. Alternating layers of chicken mixture and crumbled tortilla chips, fill casserole and top with cheese. Bake for 1 to 1½ hours or until cheese melts.

Yield: 4 servings

RASPBERRY CHICKEN

4-6	chicken breasts, boned	½	cup chicken broth
¼	cup butter	½	cup half-and-half cream
1-2	onions, sliced	½	cup raspberries
4	tablespoons raspberry vinegar		

Sauté chicken breasts in butter until browned and tender; remove from pan. Simmer onions in pan juices, covered, about 10 minutes. Add vinegar and cook until reduced and syrupy. Whisk in chicken broth and cream. Cook until reduced slightly. Add cooked chicken and heat for 5 minutes. Remove chicken. Spoon sauce on warm plates and put chicken on top. Garnish with fresh berries.

Yield: 4 servings

ST. PAUL'S SHERRIED CHICKEN

4	chicken breasts	1	tablespoon cognac
4	tablespoons melted butter	¾	cup sherry
1½	tablespoons flour	½	cup sliced mushrooms
1	cup half-and-half cream		Parmesan cheese
	Salt and pepper to taste		

Preheat oven to 350°. Brown chicken breasts in 3 tablespoons butter and remove to ovenproof casserole. Add remaining butter to saucepan with flour and cook briefly. While stirring constantly, add cream, salt and pepper. Simmer over low heat until thick. Add cognac and sherry; cook 1 minute more. Pour sauce over chicken and add mushrooms. Sprinkle Parmesan cheese on top and bake for 30 to 40 minutes until bubbly.

Yield: 4 servings

SUN-DRIED TOMATO AND FETA CHEESE CHICKEN BREASTS

4	chicken breasts, boned	4	ounces feta cheese
¼	cup olive oil	1	(3 ounce) package sun-dried tomatoes
¼	cup melted butter		Chicken broth
	Salt and ground pepper to taste		Oregano to taste
	Basil to taste		Garlic powder to taste

Sauté chicken in oil and butter; season with salt, pepper and basil. Add cheese and tomatoes and cook 10 to 12 minutes. Add enough chicken broth to make a sauce. Season with oregano and garlic powder, let simmer until done.

Yield: 4 servings

GRILLED MARINATED CHICKEN

3	garlic cloves, minced	½	teaspoon ground pepper
2½	tablespoons olive oil	1½	tablespoons chopped rosemary
2½	tablespoons Marsala wine		
½	lemon, juiced	4	chicken breasts

Mix all ingredients and spread over chicken. Marinate for 8 hours. Grill breasts and baste with marinade.

Yield: 4 servings

BOWDEN LANE BARBECUED CHICKEN

1	cup butter	2½	cups vinegar
1	cup flour	¼	cup Worcestershire sauce
½	cup ketchup	½	cup soy sauce
2	teaspoons dry mustard	6	chickens, halved
	Red pepper		

Preheat oven to 400°. Melt butter in saucepan and add flour, ketchup, dry mustard and a generous amount of red pepper. After mixing well, add vinegar, Worcestershire and soy sauce. Heat until thickened, stirring constantly. Salt chickens and place in roaster. Spoon sauce over chicken halves and bake, covered, 1 hour. Lower heat to 375°. Uncover and brown.

Yield: 12 servings

PLANTATION BARBECUED CHICKEN

3	pounds chicken pieces	6	tablespoons brown sugar
	Salt and pepper	3	tablespoons water
6	tablespoons ketchup	2	tablespoons margarine
4	tablespoons vinegar	2	teaspoons salt
2	tablespoons lemon juice	2	teaspoons prepared
4	tablespoons		mustard
	Worcestershire sauce	1	teaspoon paprika

Preheat oven to 350°. Salt and pepper chicken; place in casserole. Combine remaining ingredients in saucepan over medium heat. Thoroughly blend and simmer to boiling. Pour sauce over chicken and bake, covered, for 2 hours.

 Can be grilled after 1 hour of baking.

Yield: 4 to 6 servings

HERBED BARBECUED CHICKEN

2	3-pound chickens	1	teaspoon paprika
1	cup vegetable or olive oil	1	teaspoon minced onion
½	cup lemon juice	½	teaspoon thyme
2	teaspoons salt	1	garlic clove, minced
2	teaspoons basil		

Place chickens in casserole dish. Combine remaining ingredients and pour over chicken. Marinate at least 6 hours. Cook on grill until tender, about 1 hour, basting frequently.

Yield: 4 to 6 servings

TAR RIVER TETRAZZINI

5	pounds chicken	1	medium onion, chopped
2	tablespoons melted butter	1	(3 ounce) jar chopped pimiento
2	tablespoons flour	1	cup sliced mushrooms
2	teaspoons salt	8	ounces extra sharp Cheddar cheese, grated
2	cups milk		
1	green pepper, chopped	16	ounces spaghetti

Cover chicken with water and simmer until done, about 1½ hours. Remove chicken from pot and reserve liquid. Cool chicken and break into chunks. Whisk together butter, flour, salt and milk. Stir and cook until you have a thick white sauce. Mix in pepper, onion, pimiento and mushrooms. Cook spaghetti in chicken stock for 8 minutes; drain and toss with chicken. Add white sauce, mix well and pour into casserole. Preheat oven to 350°. Top casserole with cheese and bake, uncovered, for 30 minutes or until cheese browns a little.

 If white sauce thickens too much, thin with chicken broth.

Yield: 10 to 12 servings

BELL ROAD CHICKEN AND RICE CASSEROLE

1	cup uncooked rice	1½	cups water
1	(10½ ounce) can cream of		Salt and pepper to taste
	celery soup	4	chicken pieces
½	package dried onion soup mix		Herb seasoning

Preheat oven to 350°. Place rice in bottom of greased casserole. Top with mixture of cream of celery soup and dried onion soup mix. Add water. Salt and pepper chicken pieces and place on top. Sprinkle with herb seasoning. Cover and bake for 1½ hours.

Yield: 3 to 4 servings

CHICKEN AND SAUSAGE COLLINS

½	pound hot Italian sausage		Salt and ground pepper to
2½	pounds chicken pieces		taste
½	pound sliced mushrooms	½	teaspoon ground cayenne
1	large red bell pepper, chopped		pepper
		¼	cup finely chopped fresh
2	garlic cloves, chopped		oregano
½	cup dry white wine	16	ounces cooked pasta

Prick sausages all over with fork and brown on all sides. Drain on paper towels and slice into 1-inch pieces; set aside. Add chicken pieces to skillet, brown on both sides; remove and set aside. Add mushrooms and sauté briefly. Return sausages and chicken to skillet and add pepper, garlic, wine, salt, ground peppers and oregano. Bring to a boil; reduce heat and simmer, covered, for 20 minutes until chicken and sausages are cooked through. Serve over pasta and garnish with parsley.

 May be made ahead and refrigerated for up to 2 days. Freezes well.

Yield: 4 to 6 servings

HOMESTEAD CHICKEN SPAGHETTI

1	3-4 pound chicken Water to cover	1	(4 ounce) can chopped pimiento
8	ounces thin spaghetti	¼	green pepper, cooked and
1	(10½ ounce) can mushroom soup		diced
1	(4 ounce) can mushrooms, undrained	¼	pound blanched almonds Grated cheese

Preheat oven to 350°. Cook chicken in water until tender. Remove and discard bones and skin. Save broth. Cook spaghetti in chicken broth; drain. Combine chicken pieces, cooked spaghetti, soup, mushrooms, pimiento and green pepper. Turn into a buttered casserole. Top with almonds and cheese. Bake for 30 minutes.

Yield: 8 to 10 servings

ATHOL ROSEMARY CHICKEN

3½	pounds chicken pieces	3	tablespoons flour
½	teaspoon paprika	1	cup chicken broth
	Ground pepper to taste	2	teaspoons crumbled dried
	Oil		rosemary
1	large onion, chopped	½	cup sherry
½	pound sliced mushrooms		

Preheat oven to 375°. Sprinkle chicken with paprika and pepper. Brown chicken pieces in a small amount of oil and place in a shallow baking dish. In the same skillet, sauté onions and mushrooms until tender. Sprinkle in flour and stir thoroughly. Add chicken broth, rosemary and sherry. Cook until thickened, stirring frequently. Pour sauce over chicken. Bake, tightly covered, for 45 minutes.

Yield: 4 to 6 servings

CHICKEN ENCHILADAS

1	cup chopped onion	¼	cup all-purpose flour
½	cup chopped green pepper	1	teaspoon coriander
5	tablespoons butter	¾	teaspoon salt
1	(4 ounce) can green chilies, chopped	2½	cups chicken broth
2	cups chopped, cooked chicken	1	cup sour cream
		1½	cups Monterey Jack cheese
		12	6-inch flour tortillas

Preheat oven to 350°. Cook onion and green pepper in 2 tablespoons butter until tender. Combine with chilies and chicken; set aside. Melt 3 tablespoons butter, stir in flour, coriander and salt. Stir in chicken broth. Cook and stir until thick; cook and stir 1 to 2 minutes more. Remove from heat and stir in sour cream and ½ cup of cheese. Stir ½ cup sauce into chicken mixture. Dip each tortilla into remaining sauce to soften. Fill each tortilla with ½ cup chicken mixture. Roll up. Arrange rolls in 13x9-inch pan. Pour remaining sauce over rolls. Sprinkle with the remaining cheese. Bake, uncovered, for 25 minutes.

Yield: 6 to 8 servings

CHICKEN AND ASPARAGUS CASSEROLE

4	cups soft bread cubes	½	cup flour
1	cup grated sharp Cheddar cheese	2	teaspoons salt
½	cup melted butter, divided	¼	teaspoon pepper
2	cups cooked asparagus	3	cups milk
		2	cups chopped, cooked chicken

Preheat oven to 350°. Mix bread cubes with cheese and ¼ cup melted butter. Line baking dish with half of bread mixture; cover with asparagus. Blend flour, salt and pepper with remaining butter. Add milk and cook until thickened, stirring constantly. Add chicken and blend well. Pour over asparagus. Sprinkle with remaining bread mixture and bake for 55 minutes.

 Turkey may be substituted. Leftovers are great for this dish!

Yield: 6 to 8 servings

ACADEMY CASSEROLE

1	3-pound fryer, cooked, boned and chopped	½	cup slivered almonds
2	(10½ ounce) cans cream of chicken soup	1	tablespoon finely chopped onions
¼	cup mayonnaise	½	package herb stuffing mix
1	cup finely chopped celery		Butter

Preheat oven to 350°. Place chicken in casserole. Combine soup, mayonnaise, celery, almonds and onions; mix well. Pour over chicken. Top with stuffing mix. Dot with butter and bake for 25 to 30 minutes or until brown.

Yield: 4 to 6 servings

CURRIED CHICKEN GRANVILLE

1	5 pound hen	2	tablespoons butter
6	cups water	1	cup reserved broth
3	stalks celery with leaves	2	(10½ ounce) cans tomato soup, undiluted
	Salt and pepper to taste	3-4	teaspoons curry powder
1	small green bell pepper, chopped		Tabasco sauce to taste
2	medium yellow onions, chopped	1	cup whipping cream

Cook hen in water with celery, salt and pepper. Simmer, covered, until chicken is tender, approximately 2 hours. Remove chicken; strain and reserve broth. Cut chicken into cubes. In a large pan, sauté green pepper and onions in butter for 15 minutes. Add broth; simmer another 15 minutes. Add tomato soup and curry powder; simmer 15 minutes longer. Add chicken to sauce. Place mixture in large double boiler, partially cover and simmer for 1¼ hours, stirring often. Check for seasoning. Use Tabasco carefully as curry is hot. Just before serving, stir in cream. Serve on rice mounds. Pass condiments of your choice.

Yield: 8 to 10 servings

SAVORY CHICKEN PIE

Pie

½	pound bulk pork sausage	1	cup milk
¼	cup butter	2	cups diced, cooked chicken
⅓	cup all-purpose flour		
¼	teaspoon salt	1	(16 ounce) package frozen green peas, thawed and drained
⅛	teaspoon pepper		
1	(10½ ounce) can chicken broth		

Pastry

1	cup all-purpose flour	½	teaspoon paprika
1	teaspoon celery seed	⅓	cup shortening
½	teaspoon salt	2-3	tablespoons water

Preheat oven to 425°. Cook sausage until brown, stirring to crumble. Drain and set aside. Melt butter over low heat in 3-quart saucepan; add flour, salt and pepper, stirring until smooth. Cook 1 minute, stirring constantly. Gradually add broth and milk. Cook over medium heat, stirring constantly, until thick and bubbly. Add sausage, chicken and peas. Cook until thoroughly heated.

Pour into 4 individual 1½-cup baking dishes or an 8-inch square baking dish.

To make the pastry, combine flour, celery seeds, salt and paprika. Cut in shortening until mixture resembles coarse meal. With a fork stir in water, 1 tablespoonful at a time, to moisten dry ingredients. Shape dough into ball. Roll pastry on lightly floured surface to ¼-inch thickness in a shape slightly smaller than baking dish. Place pastry over chicken mixture. Bake for 20 to 25 minutes until crust is browned.

Yield: 6 servings

MARINATED TURKEY BREAST FILET

½	cup sherry or white wine	1-2	tablespoons minced fresh
¼	cup light soy sauce		ginger
3-4	garlic cloves, crushed	1	turkey breast filet
½	lemon, juiced		

Combine sherry, soy sauce, garlic, lemon juice and ginger; mix well. Pour over turkey breast and marinate in refrigerator for several hours or overnight. Remove from refrigerator 1 hour before grilling. Cook turkey breast on preheated grill until done, basting with marinade. Boil leftover marinade to serve over rice.

 Turkey and marinade may be frozen, then thawed to cook.

Yield: 4 servings

BAKED CORNISH HENS WITH BOURSIN

4	Cornish game hens	2	tablespoons lemon juice
1	Boursin cheese with herbs		Salt and ground pepper to
6	tablespoons butter, room		taste
	temperature	1	egg yolk

Preheat oven to 375°. Remove backbone from hens. Flatten and place, skin side up, in a large baking pan. Beat cheese with butter until blended. Beat in lemon juice; season with salt and pepper. Spread half the sauce on hens; bake for 25 minutes. Beat egg yolk into remaining cheese/butter mixture and reserve. After 25 minutes, remove hens from oven and coat with remaining sauce. Bake for 20 minutes more. To serve, place hens on a platter and cover with pan gravy.

Yield: 4 servings

ALLISON HOUSE CORNISH HENS

4	Cornish hens	⅓	cup soy sauce
1	cup melted butter	¼	teaspoon ground ginger
⅓	cup sugar	1	small onion, sliced
1	teaspoon cornstarch	1	stalk celery, chopped

Preheat oven to 350°. Thaw hens; wash and dry. Place celery and onion in cavity. Brush with butter; bake in open roaster for 1 hour, basting often with butter. Mix sugar, cornstarch, soy sauce and ginger; boil over medium heat for 1 minute until thickened slightly. Reduce oven temperature to 250°. Bake hens for 20 to 30 minutes more, basting often with mixture.

Yield: 4 to 6 servings

CRAB AND ARTICHOKE CASSEROLE

Casserole

1	(14 ounce) can artichoke hearts	1	pound backfin crabmeat
		1	cup sliced mushrooms

Cream Sauce

4	tablespoons butter		Cayenne pepper to taste
4	tablespoons sherry	½	cup breadcrumbs
5	tablespoons flour	4	tablespoons Parmesan
2	cups half-and-half cream		cheese
	Salt to taste		Paprika

Preheat oven to 400°. Halve or quarter artichoke hearts and place in a well-greased, 1½-quart shallow baking dish. Cover with crabmeat and mushrooms. Melt butter; add flour, stirring constantly. Stir in sherry, cream, salt and pepper, cooking over low heat until sauce consistency. Spread sauce over mixture. Combine breadcrumbs and Parmesan cheese; sprinkle on top. Dust with paprika and bake for 15 minutes.

Yield: 6 servings

CRAB QUICHE

1	8-inch pie crust	3	eggs
2	green onions, minced	1	cup whipping cream
3	tablespoons butter	1	tablespoon tomato paste
1	cup crabmeat	½	teaspoon salt
2	tablespoon dry white wine	1	pinch of pepper
		¼	cup grated Swiss cheese

Preheat oven to 375°. Cook crust about 5 minutes. Sauté onions in butter; add crabmeat and stir gently. Add wine. Raise heat and boil 30 seconds. Let cool slightly. Beat eggs, cream, tomato paste, salt and pepper. Blend in crab mixture and pour into pie crust. Sprinkle cheese on top. Bake for 25 to 30 minutes.

Yield: 6 servings

CRAB STUFFED JUMBO SHRIMP

1	pound backfin crabmeat	4	tablespoons chopped parsley
½	cup mayonnaise		
6	tablespoons lemon juice	¼	cup breadcrumbs
¼	teaspoon garlic salt	16	jumbo shrimp
1	tablespoon Worcestershire sauce	3	tablespoons melted butter

Preheat oven to 450°. Combine all ingredients except shrimp and butter. Peel, clean and butterfly shrimp; stuff with crabmeat mixture. Brush with melted butter and bake for 5 minutes.

Yield: 8 luncheon or 4 dinner servings

DEVILED CRAB

1	tablespoon butter	2	dashes hot sauce or ½
2	tablespoons flour		teaspoon red pepper
1½	cups half-and-half cream	1	pound backfin crabmeat
1	teaspoon salt	2	hard-boiled eggs, finely
1	teaspoon dry mustard		chopped
1	tablespoon		Buttered breadcrumbs
	Worcestershire sauce		

Preheat oven to 350°. In saucepan, melt butter and blend in flour; add cream. Cook over low heat until mixture thickens; add seasonings. Fold in crabmeat and eggs gently. Pour into small, buttered baking dish. Cover with breadcrumbs and bake for 15 to 20 minutes until crumbs are browned.

 Individual shells may be used.

Yield: 4 to 6 servings

JOCKEY'S RIDGE CRAB CAKES

1½	white bread slices	1	teaspoon Worcestershire
1	egg, beaten		sauce
1	pound backfin crabmeat		Dash Tabasco sauce
3	tablespoons Miracle Whip		Salt and pepper to taste
2	teaspoons yellow mustard		Parsley to taste
		2	tablespoons butter

Crumble bread into egg; pour over crabmeat. Combine Miracle Whip, mustard, Worcestershire sauce, Tabasco, salt, pepper and parsley. Shape into patties and refrigerate at least 4 hours prior to cooking. Fry in butter until golden brown.

Yield: 8 crab cakes

SAUCY CRAB

¼	cup butter	¾	teaspoon pepper
1	cup half-and-half cream	1	egg
1	teaspoon dry mustard	2	tablespoons minced
1	tablespoon lemon juice		pimiento
2	teaspoons Worcestershire sauce	1	pound backfin crabmeat Crushed saltines
1	teaspoon salt		

Preheat oven to 350°. Melt butter; mix in cream, mustard, lemon juice, Worcestershire sauce, salt, pepper and egg. Stir constantly until heated through. Add pimiento; mix with crabmeat and place in buttered, oblong casserole. Top with saltines and bake for 30 minutes.

Yield: 4 to 6 servings

CRAB AND WILD RICE

1	cup wild rice	2	garlic cloves, minced
1	cup butter, divided	½	cup flour
1½	cups chopped celery	4	cups half-and-half cream
1	cup chopped onions	2	egg yolks, beaten
1	cup chopped mushrooms	1	cup grated Parmesan cheese, divided
1	teaspoon thyme		
	Salt and pepper to taste	1½	pounds backfin crabmeat
3	shallots, chopped		

Preheat oven to 425°. Cook rice according to package directions. Melt half the butter; add celery, onions and mushrooms. Brown slightly; add thyme, salt and pepper to taste. Pour over cooked rice and mix. Place in a large oven-proof dish; set aside. Melt remaining butter; add shallots and garlic. Add flour and stir well. Add cream slowly. Remove from heat; stir in egg yolks and half the cheese. Beat well until smooth. Place crabmeat on top of rice. Pour sauce over crab and sprinkle with remaining cheese. Bake 25 to 30 minutes, until cheese browns and sauce bubbles.

Yield: 6 to 8 servings

CATCH OF THE DAY

2	fish - "catch of the day"	2	teaspoons lemon juice
¼	cup melted butter	¼	teaspoon pepper
½	teaspoon salt	1	teaspoon paprika
2	tablespoons grated onion		

Preheat oven to 350°. Mix all ingredients and pour over fish. Bake until fish flakes, about 15 to 20 minutes.

Yield: 2 servings

BIG FISH

1	5-pound King Mackerel	¾	cup soy sauce
¾	cup peanut oil	½	teaspoon shredded ginger
1	cup chopped green onions		root

Remove head and poach fish in water until done; drain. Remove to an ovenproof platter. Heat oil to boiling point. Combine onions, soy sauce and ginger root. Pour mixture over fish. Top with hot oil and serve.

This recipe came from New York to Hertford to Edenton. It is delicious!

Yield: 8 to 10 servings

"FISH WASH" MARINADE

2	fish - "catch of the day"	3	tablespoons crushed
½	cup olive oil		garlic
2	tablespoons Dijon	8	tablespoons fresh dill
	mustard		weed

Clean and fillet fish. Blend all ingredients and finger-pat over fish. Place in refrigerator for several hours until ready to grill, but not overnight.

Our choice of fish: grouper, tuna, dolphin or any thick game fish.

Yield: 4 fillets

FANTASTIC FISH

2-4	fish, your "catch of the day"	1	tablespoon fresh snipped rosemary
2	tablespoons olive oil	2	tomatoes, thinly wedged
2	garlic cloves, sliced	1	bunch scallions, finely chopped
	Seasoned salt to taste		
3	tablespoons fresh parsley	1	sweet pepper (red, green or yellow), thinly sliced
3	tablespoons fresh thyme		
3	tablespoons fresh oregano		

Preheat oven to 400°. Clean and fillet fish. Pour olive oil in a large baking dish; add garlic and put in oven for 10 minutes. (Now the whole world knows you are cooking something wonderful!) Remove garlic from hot oil and discard. Put fish in oil; sprinkle top side lightly with seasoned salt. Scatter herbs and vegetables on top of fish and bake for 15 to 20 minutes, depending on the thickness of the fish.

Yield: 2 to 4 servings

HERBED FISH FILLETS

2	pounds fish fillets	2-3	teaspoons basil
½	cup breadcrumbs	1	cup mayonnaise
2	cups tomatoes	1	cup grated Cheddar cheese
2	teaspoons oregano		

Preheat oven to 400°. Roll fillets in breadcrumbs and layer, side by side, in casserole dish. Peel, seed and chop tomatoes; mix with oregano and basil and spoon over fillets. Mix mayonnaise and cheese; gently spoon over tomatoes. Bake for 20 minutes.

 This is delicious!

Yield: 4 to 6 servings

CANNONS FERRY FRIED SALT HERRING

12-16 pieces salt herring fillets	**Vegetable oil**
1½ cups white cornmeal	

Soak herring 10 to 12 hours in cold water, changing water once. Remove from water, pat dry, and roll in cornmeal. Fry in oil until crisp.

 A special breakfast at St. Paul's when the herring are running!

Yield: 4 servings

TRESTLE ITALIAN TROUT

4	**whole trout**		**Salt to taste**
3	**tablespoons flour**	**1**	**cup sliced mushrooms**
¼	**cup butter**	**1**	**cup white wine**

Roll trout in flour. Heat butter on full heat in pan large enough to hold 4 fish; brown 1 minute on each side. Sprinkle salt and mushrooms on fish; add wine. Cook, uncovered, on full heat for 10 minutes.

Yield: 4 servings

PAN-BROILED SHAD

1	**shad**	**2**	**tablespoons melted butter**
	Salt to taste		**Lemon slices**
3	**tablespoons lemon juice**		

Split shad lengthwise along backbone. Salt generously and refrigerate all day or overnight. Wash and dry before cooking. Barely grease fish griddle and heat to medium hot. Lay shad in pan, skin side up, and cook slowly until golden brown. Turn shad; squeeze lemon juice and pour melted butter on golden side. Serve with lemon slices.

 Especially good with spoon bread.

Yield: 4 to 6 servings, according to size of shad

CREAM HERB SAUCE FOR GRILLED FISH

¼	cup butter		¼	teaspoon oregano
1	cup minced mushrooms		¼	teaspoon basil
¼	cup minced shallots			Pinch thyme
1	teaspoon minced garlic			Salt and pepper to taste
2	tablespoons flour		2	tablespoons minced
¾	cup whipping cream			parsley
¼	cup dry vermouth		1	tablespoon capers,
2	teaspoons lemon juice			washed and drained

Melt butter; sauté mushrooms, shallots and garlic over medium heat for 2 to 3 minutes. Blend in flour thoroughly; add cream, vermouth, lemon juice, oregano, basil, thyme, salt and pepper. Cook, stirring constantly, until mixture thickens. Add parsley and capers. Thin sauce with additional cream if desired. Serve over grilled fish of your choice.

Yield: 1½ cups sauce

EDEN ALLEY GRILLED TUNA STEAK

½	cup zesty Italian dressing		2	teaspoons lemon juice
1	teaspoon teriyaki sauce		4	1-inch thick tuna steaks
2	teaspoons soy sauce		1-2	cups white wine, optional

Mix first 4 ingredients well and pour over steaks. Marinate for 1 hour. While tuna is marinating, sip wine and heat grill. Grill steaks 4 to 5 minutes per side over medium coals.

Yield: 4 servings

GRILLED TUNA KABOBS

4	tuna steaks, cubed		¼	cup Key lime juice
¼	cup coconut rum		1	garlic clove, minced
¼	cup Triple Sec		1	(16 ounce) can pineapple
1	teaspoon fresh ground ginger			chucks, drained

Marinate tuna for 1 hour in rum, Triple Sec, ginger, lime juice and garlic. Skewer pineapple chunks and tuna on sticks and grill 5 minutes.

Yield: 4 servings

BAYSIDE FRIED OYSTERS

1	quart oysters		Salt and pepper to taste
2	eggs, beaten	1	cup saltine cracker
2	tablespoons milk		crumbs

Drain oysters. Mix eggs, milk and seasonings. Dip oysters in egg mixture and roll in crumbs. Deep fry in hot vegetable oil (375°) about 2 minutes.

Yield: 6 servings

HEWES HOUSE PANNED OYSTERS

¼	cup butter	1	teaspoon Worcestershire
1	pint oysters		sauce
			Salt and pepper to taste

Melt butter, add oysters and cook over low heat. Stir constantly until edges curl. Add Worcestershire sauce, salt and pepper. Remove from pan with slotted spoon and serve in ramekins. Use hot seafood sauce for dipping.

Yield: 2 servings

SCALLOPED OYSTERS

2	cups saltine crackers		Pepper to taste
½	cup melted butter		Half-and-half cream
2	pints oysters, reserve	¼	teaspoon Worcestershire
	liquid		sauce

Preheat oven to 350°. Coarsely crumble crackers and toss with butter; set aside. Drain oysters, reserving liquid. Spread one-third of the cracker crumbs in a greased, 2-quart baking dish. Cover with half the oysters; sprinkle with pepper. Add one-third of the crumbs to make another layer. Add remaining oysters and top with remaining cracker crumbs. Combine oyster liquid with cream to make 1 cup. Stir in Worcestershire sauce; pour over oysters. Bake for 30 to 40 minutes.

 Be careful not to overbake!

Yield: 8 servings

SALMON LOAF WITH SAUCE

Loaf

1	can Red Sockeye salmon	1½	cups breadcrumbs
4	tablespoons butter	1	cup milk
4	eggs		Salt and pepper to taste

Sauce

1	pint milk	1	tablespoon
1	tablespoon cornstarch		Worcestershire sauce
2	tablespoons butter		Cayenne pepper to taste
1	tablespoon tomato		Dill to taste
	ketchup	1	egg

Preheat oven to 350°. Drain salmon; chop fine. Combine all ingredients for loaf and season to taste; beat well. Pour into loaf pan and bake for 30 to 40 minutes.

For sauce, heat milk and thicken with cornstarch and butter. Add ketchup, Worcestershire sauce, cayenne and dill; add egg and beat well. Serve over loaf.

Yield: 1 loaf

BELL BUOY SCALLOPS

1	pound scallops		Salt and pepper to taste
2	tablespoons lime juice	1	pound bacon
½	cup melted butter	2	green peppers, cut in
4	drops Tabasco sauce		wedges
	Basil		

Marinate scallops in lime juice, butter, Tabasco sauce, basil, salt and pepper for at least 30 minutes. Wrap scallops in bacon and, alternating with green pepper, place them on skewers. Grill until the edges are black.

Yield: 4 to 6 servings

COLONY SCALLOPS

1	small onion, chopped	1	tablespoon lemon juice
3	tablespoons butter	3	tablespoons flour
1	pound scallops	½	teaspoon salt
½	pound sliced mushrooms	1	cup half-and-half cream
½	cup dry white wine		Parmesan cheese
½	cup water		Parsley

Sauté onion in butter for 5 minutes. Add mushrooms, wine, water and lemon juice. Combine flour, salt and cream; add to sauce and stir constantly until thick. Add scallops and cook an additional 5 minutes. Sprinkle cheese and parsley over each serving.

Yield: 4 to 6 servings

CABBAGE ROW SHRIMP PIE

1	pound shrimp		Salt and pepper to taste
1	small onion, minced	2	hard-cooked eggs,
1	green pepper, minced		chopped
1	tablespoon butter	½	cup grated sharp
2	bread slices, cubed		Cheddar cheese
1	(14½ ounce) can tomato	½	cup crisp breadcrumbs
	wedges, with juice		

Preheat oven to 350°. Peel and clean shrimp. Sauté onion and green pepper in butter. Add bread, tomatoes, salt and pepper; cook for 20 minutes. Add shrimp last 2 minutes of cooking. Add eggs, mix well, and place in shallow casserole. Sprinkle with cheese and breadcrumbs and bake for 15 to 20 minutes.

Yield: 6 servings

GRILLED ASIAN PESTO SHRIMP

2	pounds shrimp	1	tablespoon sherry
⅓	cup olive oil	1	teaspoon salt
1	teaspoon sesame oil	½	teaspoon ground pepper
3	tablespoons minced garlic	2	teaspoons crushed red
2	tablespoons chopped		pepper
	basil	1	tablespoon chopped
1	teaspoon chopped thyme		chives
1	teaspoon chopped		
	rosemary		

Shell and devein shrimp; refrigerate. Combine remaining ingredients and process until paste consistency. Coat shrimp with herb paste. Cover tightly and marinate 6 hours, turning or stirring twice. Soak wooden skewers in water 1 hour before grilling to prevent burning. Skewer shrimp and grill until done.

 May be sautéed or grilled.

Yield: 4 to 6 servings

CURRIED SHRIMP

1½	cups uncooked rice	1	teaspoon celery salt
1	onion, diced	2½	pounds shrimp
1¼	cups butter	½	cup slivered almonds
1	teaspoon curry powder	¾	cup raisins
1	teaspoon white pepper		

Preheat oven to 350°. Cook rice according to package directions. Sauté onion in butter and add curry, pepper and celery salt. Peel and devein shrimp. Mix with onions and add cooked rice, almonds and raisins. Place in 9x13-inch casserole and bake for 30 minutes.

Yield: 8 servings

SOUNDSIDE SHRIMP BOIL

1½	cups salt (the correct amount!)	4	packages beef sausage, cut into 2-inch pieces
1	package McCormick crab boil	4	packages frozen corn on cob
4	onions, quartered	5	pounds unpeeled shrimp

Fill a large crab pot one-third full of water. Add salt, crab boil, onions and sausage; bring to a boil and simmer 45 minutes. Add corn; bring to a boil and simmer 10 minutes. Add shrimp and cook until pink; drain and serve with tossed salad and crusty French bread.

Traditionally this is served on paper plates on a table covered with newspaper.

Hillshire Farm sausage and Green Giant Niblets corn are best.

Yield: 10 to 12 servings

SANDY POINT SHRIMP GUMBO

3	pounds shrimp	2	tablespoons all-purpose flour
½	cup mushrooms		
2	small onions, finely chopped	½	cup half-and-half cream
		2	dashes Worcestershire sauce
½	green pepper, finely chopped		
		2	dashes hot sauce
2	tablespoons butter	2	teaspoons salt
3	medium tomatoes, peeled and chopped		Pinch of pepper
		½	cup dry sherry
		½	cup buttered breadcrumbs

Preheat oven to 375°. Shell and devein shrimp. Sauté mushrooms, onions and green pepper in butter until tender. Add tomatoes; cook slowly for 8 to 10 minutes. Stir in flour and cream. Add Worcestershire sauce, hot sauce, salt, pepper, shrimp and sherry. Blend well and pour into buttered casserole; top with breadcrumbs. Bake for 10 minutes or until top is brown. Serve over rice or on top of cornbread.

Yield: 6 to 8 servings

LUNCHEON SHRIMP CURRY

Casserole

2½	pounds shrimp	4	(10½ ounce) cans cream of
1½	cups chopped onion		celery soup
1½	cups chopped celery	¾	cup sliced mushrooms
½	cup butter	2	tablespoons curry powder
2	cups applesauce	¼	teaspoon salt

Condiments

Chopped Macadamia
nuts, peanuts, cashews
Hard-boiled egg whites,
sieved
Hard-boiled egg yolks,
sieved
Raisins plumped in wine
or warm water

Mango chutney
Crumbled bacon
Chopped green onions
Pineapple chunks
Banana slices
Grated coconut

Shell and devein shrimp; halve lengthwise. Cook onion and celery in butter until almost tender. Stir in applesauce, soup, mushrooms, curry powder and salt. Add shrimp and simmer, uncovered, stirring frequently for 10 minutes. Serve over hot rice with condiments.

Yield: 10 to 12 servings

WATER STREET SHRIMP BAKE

2	cups shrimp	½	cup chopped celery
2	cups uncooked rice	¼	cup chopped pimiento
1	cup mushrooms	1	(16 ounce) can tomatoes,
¾	cup melted butter		drained
1	cup chopped green	¾	teaspoon salt
	pepper	½	teaspoon chili powder
1	cup chopped green onion	½	cup melted butter

Preheat oven to 300°. Shell, devein and cook shrimp; set aside. Cook rice according to package directions; set aside. Sauté mushrooms in ¼ cup butter until tender. Add pepper, onion, celery, pimiento, tomatoes, salt and chili powder. Stir in shrimp and rice. Place in greased, 2-quart casserole; drizzle with remaining butter and bake for about 30 minutes until hot.

Yield: 6 to 8 servings

SHRIMP SCAMPI

¾	pound medium shrimp	2	tablespoons minced parsley
6	tablespoons butter		
1	tablespoon green onion	¼	teaspoon grated lemon peel
1	tablespoon vegetable oil		
4-5	garlic cloves		Dash liquid hot pepper seasoning
2	teaspoons lemon juice		
¼	teaspoon salt		

Shell and devein shrimp; pat dry. Melt butter in frying pan over medium heat. Stir in onion, oil, garlic, lemon juice and salt. Cook until bubbly. Add shrimp and cook, stirring occasionally, until shrimp turns pink. Stir in parsley, lemon peel and hot pepper seasoning.

Yield: 2 servings

SHRIMP AND CAPERS FOR TWO

2	garlic cloves, minced		Salt and pepper to taste
¼	cup butter	¼	cup white wine
1	pound shrimp	½	small bottle drained capers
½	teaspoon thyme		
1	teaspoon lemon juice	1	teaspoon cornstarch

Sauté garlic in butter for 1 minute. Peel and devein shrimp. Add shrimp, thyme, lemon juice, salt, pepper, wine and capers. Cook, uncovered, until shrimp turns pink. Mix cornstarch with a little water to thicken mixture slightly.

Yield: 2 servings

SHRIMP CURRY

1	medium onion, chopped	⅓	cup sour cream
1	pound shrimp, peeled and deveined	2	green onions, chopped
		1	teaspoon curry powder
3	tablespoons butter		
1	(10½ ounce) can cream of shrimp soup		

Sauté onions and shrimp in butter. Add soup, sour cream, green onions, and curry powder. Heat; <u>do not boil</u>. Serve over rice.

Yield: 2 to 4 servings

SUNDAY SEAFOOD

1	cup cooked grits	2	cups sliced mushrooms
¾	cup extra sharp cheddar cheese, grated	1	cup scallions, diced
		1	large garlic clove, pressed
	Tabasco to taste		
¹⁄₁₆	teaspoon nutmeg	4	teaspoons lemon juice
	White pepper to taste		Tabasco to taste
1	pound shrimp	1	cup chopped parsley
6	slices diced bacon		Salt and pepper to taste
2	tablespoons cooking oil		

Cook grits according to package directions; add cheese, Tabasco, nutmeg and white pepper. Set aside; keep warm while preparing shrimp. Cook bacon until done but not crisp. Add enough oil to make layer of fat in pan, about one-eighth inch deep. When hot, add shrimp in even layer; turn when pink. Add mushrooms and sauté 4 minutes. Add scallions and garlic; stir briefly. Add lemon juice and dash or two of Tabasco. Remove from heat; sprinkle with salt, pepper and parsley. Divide grits among 4 plates and top with shrimp.

Yield: 4 servings

HAYES FARM SCALLOPS AND CRABMEAT

1½	cups chopped spring onions		Dash of Tabasco sauce
		1	pound sea scallops
1	cup butter	1	pound lump crabmeat
1	lemon		Paprika
2	teaspoons capers		Parsley
1	tablespoon Worcestershire sauce		

Slowly simmer onions for 10 to 15 minutes with mixture of melted butter, juice and pulp of lemons, capers, Worcestershire sauce and Tabasco sauce. Add drained scallops and sauté lightly for 5 to 7 minutes, or until scallops begin to flake; add crabmeat. Serve in shells or ramekins. Top with a sprinkle of paprika and garnish with parsley.

Yield: 6 servings

BARKER HOUSE

A familiar view of Edenton Bay includes the colonial cannons and the Barker House. The house was built around 1782 for Thomas and Penelope Barker. Mrs. Barker, an activist during the Revolution, hosted the 1774 Edenton Tea Party.

The house was purchased in 1952 by several civic organizations, moved to its present location and restored. For many years, the Barker House served as the headquarters for Historic Edenton. Today, the house continues to be an important place for civic activities and private functions.

Side Dishes

SIDE DISHES

TANN YARD ASPARAGUS

2	tablespoons flour	2	cups cooked asparagus
2	tablespoons butter	1	cup grated Cheddar
¼	teaspoon salt		cheese
¼	teaspoon pepper	2	hard-boiled eggs, sliced
1¾	cups undiluted	¼	cup coarsely chopped
	evaporated milk		almonds

Preheat oven to 350°. Stir flour into melted butter; add salt and pepper. Gradually add milk, stirring constantly, until thickened. Arrange asparagus, cheese, eggs and almonds in layers in greased 2-quart casserole. Top with white sauce and bake for 20 minutes.

Yield: 6 servings

NASTURTIUM ASPARAGUS

1	pound asparagus spears	1	tablespoon minced
6	tablespoons butter		parsley
1	tablespoon lemon juice	1	tablespoon capers
1	tablespoon white wine		Salt and pepper to taste
2	tablespoons minced		
	nasturtium flowers		

Cook asparagus until tender but still crisp. Drain and wrap in a tea towel while you prepare this tasty nasturtium sauce. Combine remaining ingredients in a saucepan and heat, being careful not to let the butter brown. Pour over asparagus.

Yield: 4 servings

MARINATED ASPARAGUS

1	pound fresh asparagus	½	teaspoon ground pepper
⅓	cup vinegar		Salt to taste
¼	cup sugar	3	whole cloves
¼	cup water	1	stick cinnamon
¼	teaspoon celery seed		

Blanch asparagus or cook in microwave for 3 to 4 minutes until tender; drain. Bring vinegar, sugar, water, celery seed, salt, cloves and cinnamon to a boil. Pour over asparagus and refrigerate for 24 hours.

Yield: 6 to 8 servings

ALBANIA ASPARAGUS HAM ROLLS

¼	cup minced onion	12	thin slices cooked buffet-
1	cup sliced mushrooms		style ham
4	tablespoons melted butter	2	(14 ounce) cans green
2	(10½ ounce) cans cream of		asparagus spears, drained
	mushroom soup	6	hard-boiled eggs,
½	cup sherry		chopped
½	cup milk		

Preheat oven to 350°. Sauté onion and mushrooms in butter until lightly golden. Add soup, sherry and milk; whisk until smooth. Wrap each ham slice around a group of 3 or 4 asparagus spears. Place side by side in a single layer in shallow casserole. Top with eggs, cover with sauce and bake for 20 minutes.

Yield: 12 servings

HAUGHTON POINT BEANS

1½	pounds fresh green beans	⅛	teaspoon pepper
2	tablespoons oil	2	tablespoons plain
1	tablespoon red wine		breadcrumbs
	vinegar	2	tablespoons grated
1	tablespoon dried minced		Parmesan cheese
	onion	1	tablespoon melted butter
¼	teaspoon salt		Paprika
1	garlic clove, finely minced		

Preheat oven to 350°. Cut beans into 1-inch pieces and cook. Toss with oil, vinegar, onion, salt, garlic and pepper. Pour into 1-quart casserole. Combine breadcrumbs, cheese and butter; pour over beans. Sprinkle with paprika and bake, uncovered, for 15 to 20 minutes until heated through.

 Great side dish to serve with meats or poultry.

Yield: 4 to 6 servings

SPEIGHT HOUSE LEMON BROCCOLI

1	bunch broccoli	1	tablespoon soy sauce
4	tablespoons unsalted butter	2	teaspoons lemon juice
			Salt and pepper to taste

Trim tough ends from broccoli and slice into florets, leaving short stems. Blanch in boiling water until crispy tender, about 2 to 3 minutes. Drain and refresh under cold water. Melt butter in large skillet over medium-high heat. Add soy sauce, lemon juice and broccoli. Stir-fry 3 to 5 minutes or until heated through. Season with salt and pepper.

Yield: 4 servings

WEST KING STREET BROCCOLI

2	packages frozen chopped broccoli	1	tablespoon grated onion
1	(10½ ounce) can cream of mushroom soup	1	(4 ounce) can water chestnuts
1	egg, beaten	½	cup breadcrumbs
½	cup mayonnaise	½	cup grated Cheddar cheese

Preheat oven to 400°. Cook and drain broccoli. Mix all ingredients except breadcrumbs and cheese; pour into casserole dish. Top with crumbs and cheese. Bake for 30 minutes.

Yield: 8 to 10 servings

BABY CARROTS BOURBONNAISE

¾	pound scraped baby carrots	2	tablespoons bourbon
⅔	cup orange juice	⅛	teaspoon salt
2	tablespoons butter	1	teaspoon fresh chopped dill
2	tablespoons brown sugar		

Cover carrots with orange juice and cook for 12 to 15 minutes. Drain and reserve juice. Combine juice, butter, sugar, bourbon and salt. Simmer, stirring, until butter melts. Do not boil. Pour sauce over carrots and sprinkle with dill.

Yield: 4 servings

CARROT JALAPEÑO MARINADE

12	peeled and diagonally sliced carrots	2	large onions, thinly sliced
1	(12 ounce) can jalapeño peppers, rinsed	1	cup oil
		1	cup white vinegar
		1	teaspoon salt

Place carrots in large bowl, cover with hot water and let stand for 30 minutes. Drain and plunge into cold water; add a few ice cubes and let stand for 15 to 20 minutes. Combine peppers with remaining ingredients. Drain carrots and add to mixture. Cover and refrigerate overnight.

 Marinade improves with age and will keep in refrigerator up to 4 months.

Yield: 10 to 12 servings

CROATAN CARROTS

3	pounds carrots	½	cup vinegar
1	medium onion	1	tablespoon prepared mustard
1	green pepper		
1	(10½ ounce) can tomato soup	1	teaspoon Worcestershire sauce
½	cup oil		Salt and pepper to taste

Peel and slice carrots, onion, and green pepper; cook in boiling water until done. Mix remaining ingredients and pour over carrot mixture. Marinate overnight or until ready to serve.

 This will keep for several weeks in the refrigerator.

Yield: 20 servings

BENNETT'S MILL GLAZED CARROTS

2	chicken bouillon cubes	1-2	medium onions
2	pounds sliced carrots	1½	tablespoons butter
2	cups water	2	tablespoons flour

Dissolve bouillon in boiling water; add carrots and cook for 15 to 20 minutes until tender. Sauté onions in butter and add to carrots. Mix flour with enough water to thicken and stir into carrots and onions.

Yield: 8 to 10 servings

CHRISTENING CARROTS

6	cups sliced carrots	½	teaspoon salt
4	tablespoons butter	2	tablespoons chopped
½	cup brown sugar		parsley
4	tablespoons yellow mustard		

Cook carrots in boiling water for 10 to 15 minutes until tender; drain and set aside. Melt butter; stir in brown sugar, mustard and salt. Mix well and add carrots, stirring constantly, until glazed. Pour into serving dish and sprinkle parsley over the top.

Yield: 8 to 10 servings

CHILI CAULIFLOWER

1	(4 ounce) can green chilies, drained	¼	cup flour
1	medium cauliflower	1½	cups milk, divided
2	cups grated Monterey Jack cheese	2	eggs, beaten

Preheat oven to 350°. Line bottom of greased 10x6-inch baking dish with chilies. Break cauliflower into florets and steam until crispy tender. Place over chilies and sprinkle with cheese. Combine flour and ½ cup milk, stirring until smooth. Add remaining milk and eggs; stir well and pour over casserole. Bake for 35 minutes until set.

Yield: 6 servings

CAULIFLOWER AND CHEESE CARTERET

1	large head cauliflower	1	tablespoon minced onion
½	teaspoon salt		Few drops hot pepper
2	hard-boiled eggs		sauce
¾	cup mayonnaise	½	teaspoon white pepper
1	teaspoon vinegar	1	tablespoon lemon juice
1	tablespoon olive oil	1	cup shredded Cheddar
1	teaspoon Worcestershire		cheese
	sauce		

Preheat oven to 400°. Salt cauliflower and simmer, covered, in 2 inches of water until tender but firm. Drain well and keep warm. Put eggs through sieve and add to mayonnaise. Blend vinegar and oil and beat with fork; add to mayonnaise. Add Worcestershire sauce, onion, hot pepper sauce, white pepper and lemon juice. Place cauliflower in baking dish; cover with mayonnaise sauce. Sprinkle with cheese and bake for 5 to 10 minutes until cheese is golden brown.

Yield: 4 servings

COTTON MILL CORN PUDDING

2	cups fresh corn	1	teaspoon salt
3	eggs	½	teaspoon white pepper
¼	cup flour	2	tablespoons melted butter
¼	cup sugar	2	cups light cream

Preheat oven to 325°. With sharp knife cut kernels off cob; scrape cob to remove pulp and milk of corn. Beat eggs vigorously. Mix flour, sugar, salt and pepper together. Stir corn into eggs; add flour mixture, butter and cream. Pour into buttered, 1½-quart casserole; place in pan of hot water and bake for 1 hour or until knife inserted in center comes out dry.

Yield: 6 to 8 servings

CRUSTY BAKED EGGPLANT

1	large eggplant	¼	cup breadcrumbs
1	teaspoon salt	1	tablespoon chopped
¼	cup flour		parsley
1	egg, beaten	2	tablespoons melted butter
2	tablespoons grated		
	Parmesan cheese		

Preheat oven to 400°. Peel eggplant and cut into ½-inch slices. Sprinkle both sides with salt; let stand 30 minutes. Rinse and pat dry. Combine Parmesan cheese, breadcrumbs and parsley; set aside. Assemble three shallow bowls (pie plates work well). Place flour in one, egg in one and cheese mixture in one. Dust each slice of eggplant with flour, dip in egg and then crumb mixture. Arrange eggplant in single layer in greased baking pan and bake for 25 minutes, turning once to brown on both sides.

Yield: 8 servings

HATCH HOUSE EGGPLANT CASSEROLE

1	large eggplant	¼	cup chopped onion
¼	cup butter	8-10	saltine crackers
	Salt and pepper to taste	1	cup grated Cheddar
2	eggs, beaten		cheese
¾	cup milk		

Preheat oven to 350°. Peel and cook eggplant in boiling water until tender; drain well and mash. Add butter, salt, pepper, eggs, milk and onions. Pour into casserole and top with crackers and cheese. Bake for 40 minutes.

Yield: 8 servings

CHEESY EGGPLANT

¼	cup oil	1	tablespoon chopped
1	medium onion, chopped		parsley
1	cup sliced mushrooms	1	cup grated Parmesan
½	green pepper, chopped		cheese
1	medium eggplant, cut in	1	cup shredded mozzarella
	1-inch cubes		cheese
1	(16 ounce) can tomatoes	2	eggs, beaten
1	teaspoon salt		

Preheat oven to 375°. Sauté onions, mushrooms and green pepper in oil for 5 minutes. Stir in eggplant, tomatoes, salt and parsley. Simmer slowly until eggplant is tender, about 25 minutes, stirring occasionally. Uncover and increase heat briefly if needed to reduce liquid. Combine cheeses and eggs. Spoon half the eggplant mixture into a 2½-quart casserole; top with half the cheese mixture. Repeat layers. Bake, uncovered, for 25 minutes.

Yield: 8 servings

EGGPLANT PARMIGIANA

1	medium eggplant	1	(8 ounce) can tomato
½	cup Parmesan cheese		sauce
¾	cup breadcrumbs	1	tablespoon Italian
1	egg		seasoning
2	tablespoons water	3-4	slices mozzarella cheese
2	tablespoons oil		

Preheat oven to 375°. Slice eggplant. Mix cheese and breadcrumbs; set aside. Beat egg with water. Dip eggplant slices into egg, then into breadcrumbs, coating each side. Fry in oil, turning once. Layer into pan with 2-inch sides; pour tomato sauce over fried eggplant. Sprinkle with Italian seasoning and bake for 30 minutes. Lay mozzarella cheese over the top and broil to melt.

 This can also be made with veal.

Yield: 4 to 6 servings

QUEEN STREET MUSHROOM CASSEROLE

1-2	pounds fresh mushrooms	½	cup sour cream
1	small onion, chopped	8	ounces grated Monterey
½	cup butter		Jack cheese
½	teaspoon garlic	8	ounces grated Cheddar
½	teaspoon pepper		cheese
5	rye bread slices		Chopped parsley

Preheat oven to 350°. Remove stems from mushroom caps and chop. Sauté onions in butter; add mushroom stems, garlic and pepper. Remove crusts from bread and cut into cubes. Combine bread, sour cream and mushroom caps with onion mixture. Place half of mixture into buttered casserole; put half of cheese on top. Repeat layer and top with remaining cheese and parsley. Bake for 20 minutes.

Yield: 8 servings

SCALLOPED OKRA

4	bacon slices	4-6	cups sliced okra
2	medium onions, chopped	4	medium tomatoes,
2	green peppers, chopped		chopped
1	garlic clove, chopped		

Cook, drain and crumble bacon; set aside. Sauté onions, peppers and garlic in bacon drippings until golden. Add okra and tomatoes and cook slowly, covered, for about 20 minutes. Season with salt and pepper to taste and serve with chopped bacon on top.

Yield: 6 servings

ONIONS AU GRATIN

2	large sweet onions		Salt and pepper to taste
1	chicken bouillon cube	½	cup breadcrumbs
¾	cup boiling water	2	tablespoons melted butter
¼	teaspoon thyme	¼	cup grated sharp Cheddar
1	tablespoon butter		cheese

Preheat oven to 350°. Cut onions into ½-inch thick slices and overlap in baking dish. Mix bouillon, water, thyme, butter, salt and pepper; pour over onions. Top with breadcrumbs, butter and cheese. Bake for 35 to 40 minutes until bubbly.

Yield: 3 to 4 servings

BEER BATTERED ONION RINGS

1	cup flour	2	tablespoons melted butter
1	teaspoon baking powder	4	medium onions
½	teaspoon salt	½	cup flour
2	eggs	1	quart cooking oil
½	cup plus 3 tablespoons beer		

Mix flour, baking powder and salt. Beat eggs slightly; add beer and butter. Stir dry ingredients into liquids and mix until smooth. Cover and refrigerate 1 hour. Peel and slice onions, separating into rings. Coat onions with flour. In large skillet, pour cooking oil to depth of 1½ inches. Heat oil to 375°. Dip floured onion rings into batter and fry 2 to 3 minutes, until brown. If batter becomes too thick, add a little more beer. Drain well on a brown paper bag.

Yield: 8 to 10 servings

VIDALIA ONION CASSEROLE

3	medium Vidalia onions, thinly sliced	¼	cup sour cream
		¼	cup melted butter
1	tablespoon chopped pimiento	1	(10½ ounce) can cream of chicken soup
2	cups grated American cheese	3	eggs
		½	cup sliced mushrooms
1	(4 ounce) can sliced water chestnuts, drained	3	cups crushed Ritz crackers
½	teaspoon paprika	½	cup butter
¼	cup mayonnaise		

Preheat oven to 350°. Arrange Vidalia onions in greased casserole. Mix next 10 ingredients; pour over sliced onions. Top with crackers and dot with butter. Bake, uncovered, for 30 to 40 minutes.

Yield: 8 servings

STUFFED BELL PEPPERS

4	bell peppers	1	teaspoon salt
½	pound ground beef	1	teaspoon pepper
1	medium onion, diced	1	cup herb stuffing mix
2	tablespoons butter		Worcestershire sauce to
2	tomatoes, chopped		taste

Preheat oven to 350°. Remove seeds from peppers and parboil for 8 minutes. Drain thoroughly. Sauté beef and onions in 1 tablespoon of butter; add tomatoes. Continue cooking for several minutes. Add salt, pepper, stuffing mix and a few dashes of Worcestershire sauce. Stuff peppers with beef/tomato mixture. Top with additional stuffing and dot with butter. Bake for 20 minutes.

 Omit beef and create a vegetarian-stuffed pepper.

Yield: 4 servings

PARSNIPS, POTATOES AND BACON

1	pound parsnips		Salt and ground pepper to
5	medium potatoes		taste
8	bacon slices	½	cup grated Cheddar
1	cup chicken broth		cheese

Preheat oven to 350°. Scrape and core parsnips. Cut into thin strips about 3 inches long. Peel potatoes and cut the same size as parsnips. Cut bacon into 1-inch pieces. Combine parsnips, potatoes and bacon in a well-greased dish. Cover with chicken broth and season with salt and pepper. Bake, covered, for 35 minutes. Sprinkle cheese on top and bake, uncovered, another 10 minutes.

Yield: 4 to 6 servings

BAKED CREAMED POTATOES

1	medium onion, finely chopped	2	cups milk
			Salt and pepper to taste
3	tablespoons chopped green pepper	6	medium red potatoes, sliced
4	tablespoons butter	¾	cup shredded Cheddar
2½	tablespoons flour		cheese

Preheat oven to 350°. Sauté onion and green pepper in butter about 5 minutes; stir in flour. Add milk gradually; stir and cook until thickened. Season with salt and pepper; add potatoes. Pour into 1½-quart casserole and top with cheese. Bake for 30 minutes or until bubbly.

Yield: 4 to 6 servings

POT-LUCK POTATOES FOR A CROWD

1	(32 ounce) package frozen hash brown potatoes	12	ounces grated Cheddar cheese
1	cup sour cream	2	cups breadcrumbs
1	(10½ ounce) can cream of chicken soup	¼	cup melted butter

Preheat oven to 350°. Combine potatoes, sour cream, soup and cheese. Top with breadcrumbs and drizzle with butter. Bake for 45 minutes.

Yield: 12 servings

POMME AU GRATIN PEMBROKE

2	baking potatoes		Salt and pepper to taste
1	tablespoon minced shallots	2	tablespoons Parmesan cheese
1	tablespoon minced garlic	1	cup whipping cream
2	tablespoons butter		

Preheat oven to 350°. Peel and thinly slice potatoes; place in water. Simmer shallots and garlic in butter in heavy saucepan over low heat for 3 to 4 minutes. Add potatoes, increase heat; simmer several minutes until potatoes are barely done. Add salt, pepper, Parmesan cheese and cream; simmer until potatoes are just coated. Place in buttered casserole and top with additional Parmesan cheese. Bake for 10 minutes until brown. Cool slightly before serving as potatoes will be easier to cut.

Yield: 4 to 6 servings

POWELL HOUSE SCALLOPED POTATOES

6-8	medium potatoes	1	cup grated sharp Cheddar cheese
1	(10½ ounce) can cream of celery soup		Salt and pepper to taste

Preheat oven to 350°. Peel and boil potatoes; remove from heat before completely done. Slice and layer in casserole dish with soup, cheese, salt and pepper. Repeat layers. Bake, uncovered, for 30 minutes.

Yield: 6 servings

ST. ANNE'S SWEET POTATOES

2	(28 ounce) cans sweet potatoes	1	teaspoon vanilla
1	cup sugar	1	cup brown sugar
2	eggs, beaten	½	cup flour
⅓	cup milk	⅓	cup melted butter
½	cup melted butter	1	cup chopped pecans

Preheat oven to 350°. Mix first 6 ingredients together with mixer until smooth and creamy. Pour into greased, 9x13-inch casserole. Mix brown sugar, flour, butter and pecans. Sprinkle on top of potatoes. Bake for 30 minutes.

Yield: 12 servings

SHERRIED RICE BAKE

1	small onion, chopped	2	cups consommé
1	garlic clove, chopped	1	cup water
2	tablespoons olive oil	½	cup sherry
1	cup uncooked rice	1	teaspoon rosemary leaves

Preheat oven to 350°. Sauté onion and garlic in oil; add rice and brown. Put in greased casserole; add consommé, water and sherry. Bake, covered, for 1 hour. Stir occasionally. Garnish with rosemary leaves.

Yield: 4 servings

GALA RICE

1	(7 ounce) package yellow rice mix	1	(8 ounce) can chopped mushrooms, drained
1	(8 ounce) can sliced water chestnuts, drained	1	(10 ounce) can consommé
1	(2 ounce) jar chopped pimientos, drained	1	(10½ ounce) can French onion soup
		½	cup butter

Preheat oven to 350°. Combine all ingredients except butter in greased 2-quart casserole. Dot with butter. Bake for 1 hour or until liquid is absorbed.

Yield: 10 servings

CURRIED RICE

1	beef bouillon cube	1	(10½ ounce) can beef
¼	cup water		consommé
1	cup uncooked minute rice	1	teaspoon curry powder
1	small onion, chopped	½	teaspoon salt
2	tablespoons butter		

Preheat oven to 350°. Dissolve bouillon cube in hot water. Sauté rice and onion in melted butter until brown. Add consommé, bouillon, curry powder and salt. Pour into casserole and bake, covered, for 45 minutes.

Yield: 4 servings

RICE AND GREEN CHILI CASSEROLE

1	cup uncooked rice	½	pound grated Monterey
2	cups sour cream		Jack cheese
⅛	teaspoon salt	1	(6 ounce) can chopped
			green chilies, drained

Preheat oven to 350°. Cook rice according to package directions. Combine rice and sour cream; season with salt. Arrange half the rice mixture in bottom of greased casserole. Layer with cheese and chilies. Add remaining rice and top with cheese. Bake, uncovered for 30 minutes.

 Good recipe for leftover rice.

Yield: 6 to 8 servings

WATERFRONT SOUR CREAM RICE

1	cup uncooked rice	1	pint sour cream
½	pound grated sharp	½	teaspoon salt
	Cheddar cheese	½	teaspoon cayenne pepper

Preheat oven to 300°. Cook rice according to package directions. Mix rice with cheese, sour cream and salt. Place in a greased 2-quart casserole and sprinkle with pepper. Bake for 15 minutes until thoroughly heated. Do not overcook!

Yield: 4 to 6 servings

PAXTON HOUSE RICE PILAF

1	medium onion, chopped	2	tablespoons soy sauce
1	medium green pepper,	½	teaspoon salt
	chopped	½	teaspoon garlic salt
½	cup mushrooms	¾	cup water
6	tablespoons butter	1	(10½ ounce) can beef
1	cup uncooked rice		consommé

Preheat oven to 325°. Sauté onion, pepper and mushrooms in butter. Add rice, soy sauce and salts; stir so it does not stick. Pour mixture into a greased 1½-quart casserole; add water and consommé. Bake for 1 hour and 15 minutes.

Yield: 4 to 6 servings

MACKEY'S FERRY SOUFFLÉ

1	cup spinach		Salt to taste
1	tablespoon chopped		Paprika to taste
	onion		Nutmeg to taste
3	tablespoons butter	½	cup grated Cheddar
3	tablespoons flour		cheese
1	cup milk	3	egg whites
3	egg yolks, beaten		

Preheat oven to 350°. Cook and chop spinach. Sauté onion in butter; stir in flour until blended; slowly stir in milk. When sauce is boiling, add spinach. Reduce heat and add egg yolks. Cook and stir for 1 minute until egg yolks thicken. Season with salt, paprika, nutmeg and cheese. Whip egg whites until stiff; fold lightly into spinach mixture. Grease a 9-inch ring mold. Fill with mixture, set in a pan of hot water and bake until firm, about 30 minutes. Unmold soufflé onto platter.

Yield: 4 servings

ACORN SQUASH FILLED WITH PEARS

3	acorn squash	2	large pears
¾	cup butter	½	teaspoon ground ginger
2	medium onions, minced	½	teaspoon ground mace
	Salt and ground pepper to	3	tablespoons brown sugar
	taste	3	tablespoons bourbon

Preheat oven to 400°. Cut squash in halves lengthwise and remove seeds. Place side by side in a baking dish with open side up. Pour one inch of water in dish and cover with foil. Bake for 25 to 30 minutes or until squash is three-quarters done. While squash is baking, heat butter; sauté onion until soft and golden. Season with salt and pepper. Peel and core pears; cut into ¼-inch cubes. Stir pears, ginger, mace, brown sugar and bourbon into onions. Cook, stirring constantly, for 3 minutes. Remove squash from oven and fill with pear mixture. Cover and bake 10 minutes longer.

Yield: 4 to 6 servings

JOHNSTON'S BRIDGE SQUASH

10	medium yellow squash	8	ounces mozzarella cheese
2	medium onions	¼	cup butter
2	green peppers		Salt and pepper to taste
3	medium tomatoes		Parmesan cheese

Preheat oven to 350°. Slice squash and parboil until tender. Slice onions and peppers into rings; slice tomatoes and grate cheese. Layer in 9x13-inch casserole twice: squash, onions, peppers, tomatoes; top each layer with mozzarella cheese, butter, salt, pepper and Parmesan. End with third layer of squash and top with Parmesan cheese. Bake, uncovered, for 30 minutes.

Yield: 12 servings

SOUTHERN SQUASH CASSEROLE

2	pounds summer squash	1½	cups grated sharp
¼	green pepper, chopped		Cheddar cheese, divided
1	large onion, chopped	1	(10½ ounce) can
¾	cup melted butter		mushroom soup
2	eggs, beaten	½	cup milk
3	bread slices, toasted	½	teaspoon salt
		¼	teaspoon pepper

Preheat oven to 350°. Cook squash until tender; drain well and mash. Sauté green pepper and onion in butter. Add squash, eggs, toast, ¾ cup cheese, soup, milk, salt and pepper. Blend well and pour into greased 2-quart casserole. Sprinkle remaining cheese on top and bake for 30 minutes.

Yield: 8 servings

TOMATO PIE

1	deep dish pie shell	½	cup diced onions
3-4	large tomatoes, sliced	½	cup mayonnaise
½	teaspoon salt	1	cup grated Cheddar
¼	teaspoon pepper		cheese
½	teaspoon basil	1	cup mozzarella cheese

Preheat oven to 425° and bake crust for 5 minutes; reduce heat to 400°. Remove from oven and arrange thick tomato slices in shell. Mix salt, pepper, basil and onion. Sprinkle over tomatoes. Mix mayonnaise and cheese; spread on top. Bake for 35 minutes. Let cool 10 minutes before slicing.

 A different and tasty way to use your over-abundant tomato crop.

Yield: 6 servings

GOVERNOR EDEN SAUTÉED CHERRY TOMATOES

4	tablespoons butter	1	teaspoon dried dill weed
2	shallots, chopped	½	teaspoon salt
4	green onions, chopped	1	large garlic clove, minced
2	tablespoons fresh parsley, chopped	3	cups cherry tomatoes

Melt butter in skillet over low heat and add shallots, green onions, parsley, dill, salt and garlic; sauté 4 or 5 minutes until tender. Add tomatoes, stirring gently, and cook for 5 to 7 minutes until a few of the skins burst. The tomatoes should be well coated with the butter/vegetable mixture. Serve immediately.

 Serve surrounded with steamed broccoli florets to make a wreath.

Yield: 6 servings

TOMATO CASSEROLE

½	cup chopped onion	½	cup sugar
½	cup chopped celery	2	tablespoons cornstarch
½	cup chopped green pepper	2	tablespoons vinegar
2	tablespoons olive oil		Salt and pepper to taste
2	(14½ ounce) cans tomato wedges	1	cup grated sharp Cheddar cheese
1	cup chopped zucchini	1	cup buttered breadcrumbs

Preheat oven to 375°. Sauté onion, celery and green pepper in olive oil. Add tomatoes, zucchini and sugar; bring to a boil. Mix cornstarch with vinegar and stir into tomato mixture; add salt and pepper. Pour into a buttered casserole dish. Combine cheese and breadcrumbs; sprinkle on top. Bake, uncovered, for 30 minutes.

Yield: 8 to 10 servings

VICTORY VEGETABLES

1	carrot	1	tablespoon chopped basil
1	yellow squash	1	tablespoon chopped
1	zucchini		thyme
1	red bell pepper	1	tablespoon chopped
1	green bell pepper		oregano
1	onion, sliced		Salt and ground pepper to
2	garlic cloves, chopped		taste
1	tablespoon olive oil		

Preheat oven to 350°. Julienne carrot, squash and zucchini into ½-inch sticks 2 inches long. Seed bell peppers and cut into sticks the same size. Blanch carrots in boiling water 3 to 4 minutes. Combine carrots, squash, zucchini, peppers, onion and garlic; place on a large sheet of foil. Dot with oil and sprinkle with herbs; fold foil over and seal. Bake about 25 minutes until vegetables are tender and crisp. Unwrap, season with salt and pepper.

 Can be cooked in microwave about 5 minutes. Add oil if desired. Always use fresh herbs when available.

Yield: 4 servings

IREDELL VEGETABLES

1	stack Ritz crackers	½	cup chopped celery
¼	cup melted butter	½	cup chopped onion
½	cup slivered almonds	¼	cup chopped green
½	cup sharp Cheddar cheese		pepper
1	(15 ounce) can shoepeg	¾	cup sour cream
	corn, drained	1	(10½ ounce) can cream of
1	(15 ounce) can French		celery soup
	green beans, drained		Salt and pepper to taste

Preheat oven to 350°. Crumble crackers and mix with melted butter and almonds; set aside. Grate cheese and combine with remaining ingredients; place in a shallow baking dish. Top with cracker mixture and bake, uncovered, for 45 minutes.

Yield: 8 servings

VEGETABLE MEDLEY

1½	cups broccoli florets	1	(8 ounce) can sliced water
1½	cups sliced zucchini		chestnuts, drained
½	cup red pepper strips	2	teaspoons chicken
¼	cup sliced green onions		bouillon granules
		4	teaspoons butter

Combine first 5 ingredients in a shallow, microwave-safe, 2-quart casserole. Sprinkle with bouillon granules and toss. Dot with butter; cover with plastic wrap and vent one corner. Microwave on high for 4 minutes, turning one-fourth turn after 2 minutes. Let stand 5 minutes before serving.

Yield: 4 servings

BAL-GRAE ZUCCHINI

3	tablespoons olive oil	1	large green pepper, sliced
8	medium zucchini squash, sliced	8	ounces grated sharp Cheddar cheese, divided
1	bunch spring onions, sliced	1	cup crumbled saltines

Preheat oven to 375°. Heat oil in large skillet; sauté squash, onions and peppers. Cover and cook over low heat until just tender. Layer vegetables and cheese in buttered casserole. Top with crumbled saltines, dot with butter and bake for 30 minutes or until lightly browned and bubbly.

Yellow squash may be used in the recipe or a mix of both. Fresh basil and parsley may be added to squash mixture as it cooks.

Yield: 6 servings

203

ZUCCHINI, YELLOW SQUASH AND PIMIENTOS

3	tablespoons pine nuts	1	tablespoon chopped fresh
3	cups zucchini		basil
3	cups yellow squash	1½	tablespoons lemon juice
¼	teaspoon chopped fresh	¼	cup olive oil
	tarragon		Ground pepper to taste
		1	(4 ounce) jar pimientos

Toast pine nuts. Cube zucchini and squash; steam for 10 minutes, until tender but still crunchy. Mix tarragon, basil, lemon juice, oil and pepper in a small jar. Shake well to blend. Place zucchini, yellow squash and pimientos in a large serving bowl and toss with dressing mixture. Sprinkle with toasted pine nuts and serve warm or at room temperature.

Yield: 6 to 8 servings

ZUCCHINI AND BASIL TOMATOES

5	small zucchini, sliced	¼	teaspoon black pepper
5	tomatoes, sliced	8	ounces grated Cheddar
2	medium onions, sliced		cheese
1	teaspoon basil	3	bacon slices
½	teaspoon salt		

Preheat oven to 350°. In a 7½x11¾-inch dish, layer half the zucchini, half the tomatoes and half the onions. Combine basil, salt, pepper and half the cheese; sprinkle over vegetables. Repeat layers and top with uncooked bacon. Cover with foil and bake for 40 minutes or until fork tender. Remove cover for last 5 minutes of cooking.

Yield: 6 to 8 servings

APPLE CRANBERRY CASSEROLE

3	cups Granny Smith apples	⅓	cup flour
2	cups fresh cranberries	1½	cups rolled oats
1	cup white sugar	1	cup chopped pecans
½	cup brown sugar	½	cup melted butter

Preheat oven to 325°. Peel and dice apples. Mix with cranberries and white sugar; pour into buttered, medium oblong baking dish. Combine brown sugar, flour, oats, nuts and butter; spread over fruit. Bake for 1 hour.

 Excellent during the holidays with turkey or ham.

Yield: 12 servings

BAKED PINEAPPLE CASSEROLE

1	(20 ounce) can pineapple chunks	3	cups shredded Cheddar cheese
½	cup sugar	24	Ritz crackers, crumbled
3	tablespoons flour	3	tablespoons melted butter

Preheat oven to 350°. Drain pineapple, reserving liquid. Mix sugar, flour and liquid until smooth; add cheese and pineapple. Pour into 11¾x7½-inch baking dish. Combine crackers and butter; spread over casserole. Bake, uncovered, for 30 minutes.

Yield: 8 to 10 servings

HOT TUTTI FRUTTI

2	(29 ounce) cans peach halves	2	cups pineapple juice
2	(20 ounce) cans pineapple chunks	1	cup butter
		4	tablespoons flour
2	(29 ounce) cans pear halves	1	cup sugar
		1	cup sherry

Drain fruit, reserving 2 cups of pineapple juice; set aside. Thicken sauce made of remaining ingredients over medium heat, until like whipped cream. Pour over fruit and let stand overnight in refrigerator. Preheat oven to 350° and bake for 35 to 40 minutes. Serve warm.

Yield: 12 servings

HOT FRUIT COMPOTE

1	(16 ounce) can sliced peaches	1	(16 ounce) jar apricots
1	(16 ounce) can dark pitted cherries	4	large macaroons
		1	(16 ounce) can cherry pie filling
1	(16 ounce) can sliced pears	¼	cup brandy
1	(20 ounce) can pineapple chunks		

Drain all fruit well. Toast and crumble macaroons. Divide in half and sprinkle first half in bottom of 9x13-inch dish. Layer fruit on top. Mix together pie filling and brandy and pour over fruit. Cover and refrigerate overnight. Remove from refrigerator 30 minutes before baking. Sprinkle on remaining macaroons. Preheat oven to 350° and bake for 30 minutes until bubbly and heated through.

Yield: 8 to 10 servings

QUEEN STREET ARTICHOKE PICKLES

1	peck Jerusalem artichokes	1	cup salt
1	gallon vinegar	12	onions, sliced
4	pounds sugar	11	red pepper pods
1	box pickling spices	¼	teaspoon alum in each jar
1	(⅝ ounce) box ground mustard		

Wash and dry artichokes. Slice and pack in jars with onions. Bring vinegar, sugar, spices (put in small bag), mustard and salt to a boil. Pour hot mixture over pickles, add 1 pepper pod to each jar, cap and seal.

 Let stand 2 weeks or more until pickles "strike through".

Yield: 10 to 11 pints

SCUPPERNONG ARTICHOKE RELISH

½	peck Jerusalem artichokes	2	teaspoons celery seed
4	large onions	1	teaspoon turmeric
5	cups white sugar	8	teaspoons salt
3	pints vinegar	1	teaspoon red pepper
2	teaspoons dried mustard		

Grind artichokes and onions to relish size. Boil remaining ingredients with ground artichokes and onions. Put in sterile jars and seal.

Yield: 12 pints

CRANBERRY WALNUT RELISH

1	pound fresh cranberries	1	cup orange marmalade
2	cups sugar	1	lemon or lime, juiced
1	cup chopped walnuts		

Preheat oven to 350°. Wash and drain cranberries; mix with sugar. Cover and bake for 1 hour; remove from oven. Reduce heat to 250° and toast walnuts for 12 minutes. Add to cranberries along with marmalade and lemon or lime juice. Stir well and chill.

Yield: 4 pints

CRANBERRY CHUTNEY

1	pound fresh cranberries	½	teaspoon ground cloves
1	cup sugar	¼	teaspoon ground allspice
½	cup brown sugar	1	cup water
½	cup golden raisins	1	cup chopped onion
2	teaspoons ground	1	cup chopped apples
	cinnamon	1	cup chopped celery
1½	teaspoons ground ginger		

Combine first 9 ingredients; cook over medium heat until juice is released from cranberries, approximately 15 minutes. Stir in remaining ingredients and reduce heat and simmer, uncovered, another 15 minutes or until thickened. Stir occasionally. Chill before serving.

Chutney will keep for 2 weeks in refrigerator stored in an air-tight container.

Yield: 4 pints

DELI MUSTARD

1	cup dry mustard	1	cup sugar
1	cup malt vinegar	4	eggs, beaten

Mix mustard and vinegar; cover and let stand overnight. Blend mustard/vinegar mixture with sugar and eggs; cook in double boiler until thick. Do not boil!

Yield: 2½ cups

PEPPER RELISH

1	bushel red and green peppers	8½	cups vinegar
		8½	cups sugar
54	medium onions	¾	cup plus 5 teaspoons salt

Chop peppers and onions in food processor. Cover with boiling water; let stand 5 minutes and drain. Add vinegar, sugar and salt; boil mixture 5 minutes. Fill hot, sterile jars and seal.

Yield: 36 pints

PEAR RELISH

6	large pears	3	cups vinegar
6	bell peppers	1	tablespoon turmeric
6	medium onions	1	tablespoon salt
1	(7 ounce) jar pimientos	1	quart sugar
	Tabasco sauce to taste	1	teaspoon ground cloves

Grind pears and pour off about one-third of juice. Grind onions and peppers, reserving all juices. Combine all ingredients in a large pot; bring to a boil and simmer for 15 minutes, stirring occasionally. Pour into hot, sterile jars and seal.

Yield: 5 quarts

CRUNCHY PILGRIMAGE SWEET PICKLES

1	gallon dill pickle chips	1½	ounces pickling spice,
2	tablespoons alum		tied in bag
5	pounds sugar	4	garlic cloves
1	quart cider vinegar		

Drain pickles, transfer to large bowl. Add boiling water to cover; add alum; let stand overnight. Drain pickles, do not rinse. In large pot boil sugar, vinegar and pickling spice bag for 10 minutes. Add pickles, bring to a boil and boil 10 to 12 minutes (until pickles are clear). Remove spice bag, let pickles and juice cool. Place a garlic clove in each quart jar, fill with pickles and juice. Seal and store 2 weeks before serving.

 Use 8 garlic cloves if making pints. Served as garnish on Pilgrimage Luncheon plates.

Yield: 4 quarts

PICKLED PEARS

3	pounds pears	1	tablespoon pickling
2	cups sugar		spices
1	cup vinegar		

Peel and quarter pears. Cover with sugar and let stand overnight. Add vinegar and spices tied in cheese cloth. Cook until tender; fill sterile jars and seal.

Yield: 4 pints

MOCK WATERMELON RIND PICKLES

4	pounds very large cucumbers	1	quart vinegar
1	gallon water	½	teaspoon salt
1	cup pickling lime	6	cups sugar
		½	box pickling spices

Wash and peel cucumbers. Remove seeds and cut into chunks; let stand in water and lime for 24 hours. Stir, drain and wash 2 times. Let stand in water 1 hour. Wash, drain and put in large pot. Mix vinegar, salt, sugar and pickling spices; pour over cucumbers and let stand overnight. Next day, cook slowly for 2 hours until cucumbers turn dark. Pack in sterile jars and seal.

 These really taste like watermelon rind pickles. The secret is to get very large cucumbers.

Yield: 4 to 5 pints

DILL PICKLES

20-25	4-inch cucumbers	¼	teaspoon chopped red pepper
	Water to cover		
⅛	teaspoon alum	1	quart vinegar
1	garlic clove	1	cup salt
1	teaspoon dill seed per quart	3	quarts water

Wash cucumbers and let stand overnight in cold water and alum. Pack in hot, sterile jars. Combine remaining ingredients and heat to boiling. Pour over pickles in jars and seal.

Yield: 4 to 5 quarts

HAYES

A short distance across Queen Anne Creek and overlooking Edenton Bay is Hayes Plantation, built by James Cathcart Johnston around 1810. Hayes, a National Historic Landmark, is a mansion of great interest and beauty. A striking part of the house is the water-side porch which is connected to pedimental wings by curved colonnades. The wings house the library, which contains an extensive collection of historic leather bound books, and the kitchen which holds a vast assortment of antique cooking utensils.

The view from the porch calls to mind the many generations who have enjoyed the beauty of land and water at Hayes.

Sweets

SWEETS

APPLE WALNUT CAKE

Cake

1	can apple pie filling	2	eggs
2	cups flour	1	teaspoon vanilla
1	cup sugar	⅔	cup oil
1½	teaspoons baking soda	1	cup chopped nuts,
1	teaspoon salt		divided

Topping

1	cup sugar	½	teaspoon baking soda
½	cup sour cream		

Preheat oven to 350°. Spread pie filling in 13x9-inch pan. Combine dry ingredients and sprinkle over pie filling. Beat together eggs, vanilla, oil and ¾ cup of nuts. Mix well and pour over ingredients in pan. Stir well. Bake for 40 to 50 minutes.

Combine sugar, sour cream and baking soda in saucepan. Cook over medium heat, stirring constantly, until it comes to a boil. Prick cake all over with a fork; pour hot topping over cake and sprinkle with remaining nuts.

Cherry or peach pie filling can be substituted for apple. Top each serving with whipped cream.

Yield: 12 to 16 servings

BRAZILIAN FRUIT CAKE

1½	pounds Brazil nuts	¾	cup sugar
1	pound pitted dates	½	teaspoon baking powder
1	cup drained maraschino	½	teaspoon salt
	cherries	3	eggs
¾	cup flour	1	teaspoon vanilla

Preheat oven to 300°. Grease 9x5x3-inch loaf pan. Combine nuts, dates and cherries in bowl; mix dry ingredients and toss with fruit and nuts. Beat eggs and vanilla well; pour into bowl. Mix well and pour batter into loaf pan. Bake for 1 hour and 45 minutes.

Can use 2 small loaf pans and bake for 1 hour and 15 minutes.

Yield: 1 regular loaf or 2 small loaves

215

BAKED CHEESE CAKE

Crust

1	package Pepperidge Farm Bordeaux cookies	2	tablespoons melted butter

Filling

4	(8 ounce) packages cream cheese	6	eggs
		16	ounces sour cream
2	cups sugar	2	teaspoons vanilla

Preheat oven to 325°. Finely crush cookies; mix with butter and press in bottom of 12 inch springform pan.

For filling, mix cream cheese and sugar with electric mixer; add eggs, sour cream and vanilla. Pour into pan over crust. Bake for 45 minutes; turn oven off and leave cake in oven for 1 hour. Chill completely before serving.

Yield: 12 to 16 servings

CAYMAN CARROT CAKE

Cake

2¼	cups flour	2	teaspoons vanilla
2	teaspoons cinnamon	3	eggs, beaten
¼	teaspoon nutmeg	2	cups shredded carrots
¼	teaspoon allspice	2	cups flaked coconut
2	teaspoons baking soda	1	(8 ounce) can crushed
1	teaspoon salt		pineapple
2	cups sugar	1	cup pecans
1¼	cups vegetable oil	1	cup raisins

Icing

12	ounces cream cheese	1-2	tablespoons milk
1	teaspoon vanilla	3-4	cups powdered sugar

Preheat oven to 350°. In medium bowl, mix first 6 ingredients. In large bowl, mix sugar, oil and vanilla; gradually add flour mixture and beat in eggs. Stir in remaining ingredients and mix well. Pour into 3 well-greased 9-inch cake pans and bake for 35 to 40 minutes. Cool on racks.

Cream icing ingredients and spread over cake. Store in refrigerator.

Yield: 3-layer cake

PORCH PARTY CAKE

Cake

2	cups sifted flour	6	tablespoons cocoa
2	cups sugar	½	cup buttermilk
½	teaspoon salt	1	teaspoon baking soda
½	cup butter	2	eggs
½	cup oil	1	teaspoon vanilla
1	cup water		

Frosting

½	cup butter	1	box confectioner's sugar
6	tablespoons evaporated milk	1	teaspoon vanilla
		2	tablespoons cocoa

Preheat oven to 350°. Sift together flour, sugar and salt. Bring butter, oil, water and cocoa to a boil. Stir cocoa mixture into flour mixture. Combine buttermilk and soda; let sit for a minute. Add eggs and vanilla; blend until smooth. Pour into greased and floured 18x12x1-inch pan. Bake for exactly 20 minutes.

For frosting, melt butter and add milk, sugar, vanilla and cocoa. Blend until smooth. Spread frosting over cake. Cool, cut and remove cake from pan.

Yield: 35 servings

CHOCOLATE ECLAIR CAKE

Filling

2	packages instant vanilla pudding	8	ounces Cool Whip
3	cups cold milk	1	box graham crackers

Icing

⅓	cup cocoa	½	cup butter
¼	cup evaporated milk	1	teaspoon vanilla
1	cup sugar		

Combine pudding and milk until thick; fold in Cool Whip. In 9x13-inch dish, layer whole graham crackers and filling, beginning and ending with graham crackers.

For icing, boil cocoa, milk and sugar. Allow to cool for a minute; add butter and vanilla. Mix thoroughly and pour over cake.

Yield: 12 servings

CHOCOLATE CHEESE CAKE

Crust

1½	cups crushed vanilla wafers	⅓	cup cocoa
½	cup powdered sugar	⅓	cup melted butter

Cake

3	(8 ounce) packages soft cream cheese	4	eggs
1	(14 ounce) can sweetened condensed milk	1	(12 ounce) bag semi-sweet chocolate chips, melted
		2	teaspoons vanilla

Preheat oven to 350°. Combine crust ingredients and press in bottom and sides of a greased, 9-inch springform pan.

Beat cream cheese until fluffy. Gradually beat in condensed milk until smooth. Add remaining ingredients and mix well. Pour mixture over crust. Bake for 1 hour or until center is set. Cool for a few hours and refrigerate.

 This is very rich and very delicious!

Yield: 12 servings

FUDGE ICE CREAM CAKE

48	Oreo cookies, crushed	1	(16 ounce) can Hershey's syrup
½	cup melted butter		
½	gallon vanilla ice cream, softened	½	cup butter
		8	ounces Cool Whip
1	(14 ounce) can Eagle Brand milk	1	cup chopped nuts

Blend cookies with butter and press into a greased, 9x13-inch pan. Freeze for 30 minutes. Spread ice cream over cookie layer; freeze for 30 minutes. Heat milk, syrup and butter; bring to a boil, stirring constantly for 5 minutes. When cool, pour over ice cream; freeze 30 minutes. Spread Cool Whip over syrup mixture; freeze 30 minutes. Sprinkle with chopped nuts and freeze until ready to serve.

Yield: 12 servings

GERMAN CHOCOLATE CAKE

Cake

1	(4 ounce) package Baker's German chocolate	2¼	cups sifted all-purpose flour
½	cup boiling water	1	teaspoon baking soda
1	cup butter	½	teaspoon salt
2	cups sugar	1	cup buttermilk
4	egg yolks	4	egg whites, stiffly beaten
1	teaspoon vanilla		

Frosting

1	cup evaporated milk	1	teaspoon vanilla
1	cup sugar	1⅓	cups flaked coconut
3	egg yolks, slightly beaten	1	cup chopped pecans
½	cup butter		

Preheat oven to 350°. Melt chocolate in boiling water; cool. Cream butter and sugar until fluffy. Add yolks, one at a time, beating well after each addition. Blend in vanilla and chocolate. Sift flour with baking soda and salt; add alternately with buttermilk to chocolate mixture, beating after each addition until smooth. Fold in egg whites. Pour into 3 lined, 9-inch round baking pans. Bake for 30 to 35 minutes; cool.

For frosting, combine first 5 ingredients in pan and cook over medium heat until thickened, about 12 minutes. Add coconut and pecans and cool until thick enough to spread, beating occasionally. Frost tops of cakes and stack layers.

Yield: 1 3-layer cake

GALE STREET PINEAPPLE NUT CAKE

½	cup butter	½	teaspoon salt
1	cup white sugar	1	(15 ounce) can crushed
¾	cup brown sugar		pineapple, undrained
2	eggs	1	can flaked coconut
2½	cups flour	1	cup chopped pecans
1	teaspoon baking soda	1	teaspoon vanilla
1	teaspoon baking powder		Rum

Preheat oven to 350°. Cream butter and sugars. Beat in eggs, one at a time. Sift dry ingredients together and add gradually to mixture. Add remaining ingredients; mix thoroughly. Pour into 2 greased loaf pans and bake for 45 to 60 minutes. Watch carefully after 45 minutes so loaves do not get too brown. Cool and, if desired, flood cakes with rum. Wrap well.

Yield: 2 loaves

OAKUM STREET ORANGE CAKE

Cake

1	package yellow cake mix	4	eggs
1	(11 ounce) can mandarin	½	cup oil
	oranges, undrained		

Topping

1	(15 ounce) can crushed	1	(3¾ ounce) package
	pineapple, undrained		vanilla instant pudding
1	(9 ounce) carton Cool		mix
	Whip, thawed		

Preheat oven to 350°. Combine cake mix, oranges, eggs and oil. Beat well and pour into 3 greased 8-inch cake pans. Bake for 20 to 25 minutes. Cool.

Combine pineapple, Cool Whip and pudding mix. Beat well and ice cake. Chill.

Yield: One 3-layer cake

ALL SAINTS POUND CAKE

1	cup butter	4	cups sifted flour
½	cup Crisco	½	teaspoon salt
3	cups sugar	1	teaspoon baking powder
6	eggs	1	cup milk
1	teaspoon vanilla		

Cream butter, Crisco and sugar; beat eggs in one at a time. Add vanilla. Sift dry ingredients together. Add flour mixture and milk alternately, ending with flour. Grease and flour a large tube pan (approximately 4¼ inches deep). Pour batter into pan and put into a cold oven. Set oven to 300° and cook for 1½ hours. Raise temperature to 350° and cook 10 minutes longer. Let cool in pan 10 minutes before removing.

Yield: 12 to 16 servings

ORANGE BLOSSOMS

Blossoms

3	eggs	1½	cups flour
1½	cups sugar	1½	teaspoons baking powder
½	cup water	½	teaspoon salt
½	teaspoon vanilla		

Glaze

4	cups confectioner's sugar, sifted	2	orange rinds, grated
		1	lemon, juiced
1	lemon rind, grated	2	oranges, juiced

Preheat oven to 350°. Beat eggs with sugar; add water and vanilla. Sift together flour, baking powder and salt; blend with liquid ingredients. Fill greased mini muffin tins three-fourths full and bake for 15 to 20 minutes.

Mix glaze ingredients while muffins are cooking. Remove cupcakes from pan while hot and dip in glaze. Drain on racks over waxed paper.

Yield: 24 cupcakes

SHROVE TUESDAY CAKE

Cake

2	cups flour	½	cup butter
2	cups sugar	½	cup buttermilk
1	cup oil	2	eggs
1	cup water	1	teaspoon baking soda
4	tablespoons cocoa	1	teaspoon vanilla

Icing

½	cup butter	1	box confectioner's sugar
6	tablespoons milk	1	teaspoon vanilla
4	tablespoons cocoa	1	cup chopped nuts

Preheat oven to 350°. Mix flour and sugar. Bring oil, water, cocoa and butter to boil. Add to flour mixture and beat. Add buttermilk, eggs, baking soda and vanilla; mix well. Pour into a large rectangular pan sprayed with cooking spray. Bake for 30 minutes.

For icing, mix first 4 ingredients and beat until smooth. Add vanilla and nuts. Ice cake while hot.

Yield: 12 servings

TOFFEE BAR CAKE

2	cups flour	1	egg
1	teaspoon salt	1	cup milk
1	teaspoon baking soda	1	teaspoon vanilla
2	cups brown sugar	½	cup chopped nuts
½	cup butter	6	chopped Heath bars

Preheat oven to 350°. Thoroughly mix flour, salt, soda and brown sugar. Cut in butter. Remove 1 cup of this mixture and set aside for topping. Add to remaining mixture the egg, milk and vanilla. Pour into a greased 9x12-inch pan. Sprinkle top of cake with half the crumb mixture, Heath bars, nuts, and remaining crumb mixture. Bake for 35 minutes.

Yield: 12 servings

SNOW ON THE MOUNTAIN

Cake

4	eggs	¼	teaspoon salt
1	cup sugar	2	teaspoons vanilla
½	cup flour	1	cup walnuts
1	teaspoon baking powder	1	cup chopped dates

Fruit layer

4	cans mandarin oranges, drained	¼	cup sugar
3-4	bananas, sliced	1	pint whipping cream
		1	can coconut

Preheat oven to 350°. Beat eggs until thick; gradually add sugar. Add sifted dry ingredients. Stir in vanilla, nuts and dates. Pour into 2 greased 9-inch pans and bake for 30 minutes. Let cool. Break cake into bite-sized pieces. On a silver tray, arrange pieces of torn cake in a large circle. Mix oranges and bananas with sugar. Make a layer of fruit, then a layer of cake; make each layer smaller than the one before, so that you are shaping layers into a mountain as you go. Refrigerate. About 2 hours before serving, whip cream and cover cake. Sprinkle with coconut. Refrigerate until ready to serve.

 Cake may be made the day before. Beautiful made for a bridal shower.

Yield: 16 to 18 servings

SPICY PRUNE CAKE

Cake

1½	cups sugar	1	teaspoon nutmeg
1	cup oil	1	teaspoon allspice
3	eggs	1	teaspoon cinnamon
2	cups flour	1	cup mashed, cooked
½	teaspoon baking soda		prunes
½	cup buttermilk	1	cup chopped nuts
½	teaspoon salt	1	teaspoon vanilla

Glaze

½	cup butter	½	cup buttermilk
1	cup sugar		

Preheat oven to 350°. Cream sugar, oil and eggs. Combine flour and baking soda with buttermilk. Add to sugar mixture. Add salt and spices; fold in prunes, nuts and vanilla. Pour into a greased tube pan and bake for 1 hour.

For glaze, combine butter, sugar and buttermilk in saucepan; boil for 3 minutes. Loosen sides of cake from pan and pour glaze over warm cake. Remove from pan when cool.

 Very moist. Keeps well.

Yield: 12 to 16 servings

BOURBON BALLS

1	cup crushed vanilla wafers	1	cup confectioner's sugar
		¼	cup corn syrup
1	cup finely chopped pecans	¼	cup bourbon

Mix all ingredients thoroughly and roll into balls. Roll in confectioner's sugar.

Yield: 3 dozen

SOUTH MOSELEY STREET FUDGE

2	cups sugar	2	tablespoons white Karo
1	cup brown sugar		syrup
3	ounces unsweetened	1	pinch salt
	chocolate	2	tablespoons butter
1	cup evaporated milk	1	teaspoon vanilla
			Nuts, optional

Mix the first 6 ingredients together in a heavy pot; heat until sugar dissolves and chocolate melts. After candy gets to soft boil stage, add butter and vanilla. Let pot stand in cold water until cool. Beat with an electric mixer and stir in nuts. Turn out onto a cookie sheet. Let cool and cut into squares.

Yield: 36 pieces

CAPPUCCINO TRUFFLES

12	ounces semi-sweet	1½	tablespoons instant
	chocolate pieces		espresso or instant coffee
6	tablespoons chopped		powder
	butter		Cocoa powder,
3	tablespoons whipping		confectioner's sugar or
	cream		chopped nuts

Cook first four ingredients over medium heat, stirring until smooth. Freeze for 1 hour or until firm. With buttered hands, shape tablespoon-fuls of mixture into balls. Roll in cocoa powder, confectioner's sugar or chopped nuts. Refrigerate.

 After shaping, freeze truffles until firm, then dip in melted chocolate.

Yield: 24 truffles

TOFFEE CANDY

1	cup butter	1	cup melted semi-sweet
1¼	cups sugar		chocolate chips
¼	cup water	1	cup chopped nuts

In heavy saucepan place butter, sugar and water and cook slowly over medium heat until mixture turns a rich golden brown. (320° on candy thermometer.) Line a jelly roll pan with buttered foil. When toffee mixture is ready, pour into foil-lined pan and let set until solid but still warm. Spread half of the melted chocolate over toffee and sprinkle on half the nuts. Put in refrigerator until chocolate is hard. Take out of refrigerator, invert and peel off foil. Spread remaining chocolate and nuts on other side. Refrigerate until firm. Break into chunks and store in air tight container.

THE BEST CHOCOLATE CHIP COOKIES

1	cup softened butter	2	cups flour
1	cup brown sugar	1	teaspoon baking soda
¾	cup sugar	1	teaspoon salt
2	eggs	1½	cups semi-sweet chocolate
1	teaspoon vanilla		chips

Preheat oven to 350°. Mix together butter, sugars, eggs and vanilla; set aside. Sift together flour, baking soda and salt. Combine with butter mixture. Mix well by hand. Add chocolate chips. Drop by spoonfuls onto sprayed cookie sheet. Bake for 10 minutes. Remove while still hot and place on waxed paper to cool.

BUTTER PECAN FINGERPIE SQUARES

Crust

1¼	cups all-purpose flour	½	cup softened butter
⅓	cup sugar		

Filling

⅔	cup sugar	2	tablespoons flour
¾	cup honey	¼	teaspoon salt
2	eggs	1½	teaspoons vanilla
2	tablespoons melted butter	1	cup chopped pecans

Preheat oven to 375°. Mix crust ingredients in mixing bowl; scrape sides often. Mix until it resembles small peas. Press into 9-inch square pan. Bake for 10 minutes.

For filling, blend first 7 ingredients in a mixing bowl and mix at low speed until well blended. Stir in pecans. Pour over crust. Lower temperature to 350° and bake for 20 to 25 minutes until golden brown and filling is set in the center. Cool and cut into squares. Keep refrigerated.

Yield: 12 squares

CHOCOLATE CHEWS

½	cup shortening	2	cups sifted flour
1⅔	cups sugar	2	teaspoons baking powder
2	teaspoons vanilla	½	teaspoon salt
2	eggs	⅓	cup milk
2	squares unsweetened chocolate, melted	½	cup chopped nuts
			Powdered sugar

Cream shortening and sugar. Add vanilla, eggs and chocolate. Stir in flour sifted with baking powder and salt. Slowly pour in milk and mix thoroughly. Add nuts and chill dough. Make small balls (about 1 inch in diameter). Roll in powdered sugar. Preheat oven to 350° and bake for 12 to 15 minutes. Give them plenty of room on the baking sheet as they pop open and are very pretty.

Yield: 3 dozen

KISSIN' COUSIN BROWNIES

1	cup butter	1	cup flour
4	squares unsweetened chocolate	2	teaspoons vanilla
		¼	teaspoon salt
2	cups sugar	1½	cups chopped pecans
4	eggs		

Preheat oven to 325°. Melt butter and chocolate; cool. Mix remaining ingredients in a bowl until blended. Add butter and chocolate mixture. Bake in 9x13-inch, greased baking pan for 35 to 40 minutes.

Yield: 3 dozen

FRUIT CAKE COOKIES

1	cup butter	½	pound candied pineapple
2	cups sugar	¼	pound candied cherries
5	large eggs	½	package figs
½	cup molasses	1	package pitted dates
1¼	cups flour	1	large apple
1	teaspoon cinnamon	½	pound pecans
1	teaspoon cloves	½	pound almonds
1	teaspoon nutmeg	1	pint chopped candied fruit
1	teaspoon mace		
½	cup apple brandy	1	cup flour
1	pound raisins		

Preheat oven to 350°. Cream first 3 ingredients. Add molasses and flour. Combine spices with brandy and add to mixture. Cut up fruit and nuts. Dredge in 1 cup flour; mix well. Add to batter. Drop by teaspoonfuls onto cookie sheet. Bake for 8 to 10 minutes or until brown. Let cool a minute before removing from sheet.

 These freeze well.

Yield: 3 dozen

FRENCH ALMOND MERINGUES

1	cup granulated sugar	¼	teaspoon vanilla extract
½	cup water	½	cup ground, blanched
2	egg whites		almonds
⅛	teaspoon almond extract		

Preheat oven to 250°. Boil sugar with water to 265° (hard, almost brittle, ball). Beat egg whites until stiff; pour in the sugar syrup in a fine stream, beating constantly. When mixture holds its shape, fold in extracts and almonds. Drop by teaspoonfuls onto well greased cookie sheet and bake for 25 minutes. Turn oven off and leave cookies in oven until cool.

 Don't try these in humid weather!

Yield: 4½ dozen

ANGEL BITES

¾	cup butter	2	teaspoons vanilla
¼	cup confectioner's sugar	2	cups sifted flour
2	tablespoons cold water	1	cup chopped pecans

Preheat oven to 350°. Mix all ingredients together. Shape like little fingers. Bake on greased cookie sheet for 30 minutes. While still warm, roll in confectioner's sugar.

Yield: 2 dozen

SHORTBREAD COOKIES

1	cup softened butter	2	cups flour
½	cup sugar		

Preheat oven to 250°. Cream butter and sugar. Add flour and mix well. Break off small pieces and roll into balls and place 2 inches apart on cookie sheet. Flatten with bottom of jelly glass. Bake for 50 to 60 minutes. The cookie will be very light in color.

Yield: 3 dozen

GRANDMOTHER'S ICE BOX COOKIES

1	cup brown sugar	1	teaspoon cinnamon
1	cup white sugar	1	teaspoon baking soda
1¼	cups butter	1	teaspoon cloves
3	eggs	1	teaspoon nutmeg
4½	cups flour	1	cup nuts
½	teaspoon salt		

Preheat oven to 375°. Cream sugars and butter; add eggs. Sift flour, salt, cinnamon, baking soda, cloves and nutmeg together; add to egg mixture. Mix well. Add nuts and blend well. Shape into a long roll and leave in refrigerator, wrapped in waxed paper, for 24 hours. Slice and bake on well greased cookie sheet 10 to 12 minutes.

Yield: 4 dozen

PENELOPE BARKER LACE COOKIES

1	cup quick oatmeal	½	teaspoon salt
1	cup sugar	1	egg, beaten
3	tablespoons flour	1	teaspoon vanilla
¼	teaspoon baking powder	½	cup melted butter

Preheat oven to 325°. Mix first 5 ingredients. Add egg, vanilla and butter. Mix well. Drop ½ teaspoon of batter about 2 inches apart on foil-lined (shiny side up) cookie sheets. Bake for 8 to 10 minutes until lightly browned. Watch carefully to prevent over cooking. Cool slightly on foil on cake racks. Carefully peel from foil when cool enough to handle.

 So simple that children love to help make them.

Yield: 3 dozen

BLUEBERRY BUCKLE

Cake

¼	cup butter	½	teaspoon salt
¾	cup sugar	2	teaspoons baking powder
1	egg, beaten	½	cup milk
2	cups flour	2	cups blueberries

Topping

½	cup sugar	1	teaspoon cinnamon
⅓	cup flour	¼	cup butter

Preheat oven to 350°. Cream butter and sugar; add egg. Combine flour, salt and baking powder. Alternately add milk and flour mixture. Fold in blueberries; pour into greased and floured 9x9-inch pan.

Mix topping ingredients until crumbly and spread on top. Bake for 40 minutes.

Yield: 8 servings

CHOCOLATE CHESS PIE

1	square unsweetened chocolate	1	cup sugar
		1	teaspoon vanilla
½	cup butter	1	9-inch pie shell
2	eggs		

Preheat oven to 350°. Melt chocolate and butter together in double boiler. In separate bowl beat eggs, sugar and vanilla. Combine with melted ingredients and pour into uncooked pie shell. Bake for 25 minutes.

 An old Edenton favorite.

Yield: 6 to 8 servings

CHOCOLATE KAHLUA MOUSSE

6	ounces semi-sweet chocolate bits	¼	cup sugar
2	tablespoons Kahlua	1	cup heavy whipping cream
1	tablespoon orange juice		Whipped cream
2	eggs plus 2 egg yolks		Chocolate shavings
½	teaspoon vanilla		

Melt chocolate bits in Kahlua in top of double boiler. In blender, mix orange juice, eggs, egg yolks, vanilla and sugar. Add melted chocolate mixture. Add cream and blend again. Pour into serving dishes and refrigerate 4 to 6 hours. Serve with additional whipped cream and chocolate shavings.

 Nice for bridge club luncheons.

Yield: 6 to 8 servings

GALLERY CHOCOLATE PIE

Filling

2	squares semi-sweet chocolate	3	egg yolks
⅔	cup sugar	1	tablespoon butter
¼	cup cornstarch	1	teaspoon vanilla
2	cups milk	1	9-inch pie shell, baked

Meringue

3	egg whites	6	tablespoons sugar
¼	teaspoon salt		

Preheat oven to 350°. Melt chocolate in double boiler. Mix sugar, cornstarch, milk and egg yolks; add to chocolate. Add butter and cook over hot water until thick, stirring constantly. Add vanilla; pour into baked pie shell.

Beat egg whites with salt until stiff. Slowly add sugar and beat until mixture holds a peak. Spread on top of pie; bake for 15 minutes or until meringue is lightly browned.

Yield: 6 to 8 servings

QUICK FRUIT COBBLER

1	cup self rising flour		Dash of salt
2	cups sugar, divided	½	cup butter
½	cup milk		Whipped cream or ice
4	cups sliced fresh peaches		cream

Preheat oven to 350°. Mix together flour, 1 cup sugar and milk; set aside. In a saucepan mix fruit, remaining sugar and a dash of salt. Heat fruit mixture until hot and sugar melts. Melt butter in a 7x11-inch baking dish. Pour flour mixture into dish. Pour hot fruit evenly over flour mixture. Do not stir. Bake for 30 to 40 minutes. Serve warm with whipped cream or ice cream.

 So good! Make it often when peaches are in season.

Yield: 10 to 12 servings

OLD FISH HATCHERY FRESH STRAWBERRY PIE

1	cup sugar	½	cup water
3	tablespoons cornstarch	1	9-inch pie shell
1	quart fresh strawberries		Whipped cream

Put sugar and cornstarch into saucepan; add ½ cup of berries and the water. Cook until clear. Place remaining berries in baked pie crust; pour mixture over berries and chill. Serve with whipped cream.

Yield: 6 servings

HERSHEY BAR PIE

½	pound Hershey bars with almonds	1	9-inch graham cracker pie crust
8	ounces Cool Whip		Slivered almonds

Melt Hershey bars in a double boiler. Fold in Cool Whip, blend well and pour into pie crust. Top with almonds and chill.

Yield: 6 to 8 servings

SILK DAMASK PIE

1	baked pie shell	1	teaspoon vanilla
½	cup butter	2	eggs
½	cup sugar		Whipped cream
1	1-ounce square unsweetened chocolate		

Cream butter and sugar until light and fluffy. Melt chocolate; add vanilla. Beat thoroughly until smooth. Add eggs, one at a time, beating after each addition. Pour into baked pie shell. Cover with whipped cream. Chill for at least one hour.

Yield: 6 servings

MACAROON PIE

14	saltine crackers	1	teaspoon baking powder
½	cup chopped pecans	1	teaspoon almond extract
12	chopped dates	3	egg whites, room
1	cup sugar		temperature
¼	teaspoon salt		

Preheat oven to 300°. Roll crackers between waxed paper until finely crushed. Mix all ingredients except egg whites. Beat egg whites and fold into mixture. Pour into a well buttered 9-inch pie pan and bake for 45 minutes.

Yield: 4 to 6 servings

GRASSHOPPER PIE

1	jigger white cream de cocoa	⅔	cup milk
1	jigger creme de menthe	1	cup whipping cream
24	large marshmallows	1	9-inch pie shell, baked and chilled

Thoroughly chill the 2 liqueurs. Combine marshmallows and milk in double boiler and heat until marshmallows are melted, stirring often. Cook for 3 minutes; cool. Whip cream until quite stiff and fold into marshmallow mixture. Fold in chilled liqueurs, mixing thoroughly. Spoon into pie shell. Refrigerate 4 hours or longer before serving.

Yield: 6 to 8 servings

PUMPKIN CHIFFON PIE

3	egg yolks, beaten	½	teaspoon nutmeg
¾	cup brown sugar	1	envelope unflavored
1½	cups cooked pumpkin		gelatin
½	cup milk	¼	cup cold water
½	teaspoon salt	1	cooked pie crust
1	teaspoon cinnamon		Whipping cream

Combine egg yolks, brown sugar, pumpkin, milk, salt, cinnamon and nutmeg. Cook in double boiler until mixture thickens, stirring constantly. Soak gelatin in cold water; stir into hot mixture. Pour into cooked pie shell and chill until set. Garnish with whipped cream over entire pie.

Yield: 6 servings

LEMON MERINGUE PIE

Filling

7	tablespoons cornstarch	½	cup fresh lemon juice
1½	cups sugar	1	teaspoon grated lemon
¼	teaspoon salt		rind
1½	cups hot water	2	tablespoons butter
3	egg yolks, beaten	1	9-inch baked pie crust

Meringue

3	egg whites, room temperature	1	teaspoon fresh lemon juice
6	tablespoons sugar		

Preheat oven to 350°. In a saucepan mix cornstarch, sugar and salt. Add hot water gradually and cook for 6 to 8 minutes over direct heat, stirring constantly until thick and clear. Remove from heat. Stir ½ cup of the hot mixture gradually into beaten egg yolks. Pour back into pan and cook over low heat for 6 minutes, stirring constantly. Remove from heat and add lemon juice, rind and butter. Cool and pour into baked pie crust.

For meringue, beat egg whites until they stand in soft peaks. Gradually add sugar and lemon juice beating until firm and glossy white. Spread meringue on filling, beginning at the center and spreading to touch the crust. Bake for 15 minutes or until lightly browned.

Yield: 6 to 8 servings

WALNUT PUMPKIN PIE

1	envelope unflavored gelatin	1	teaspoon pumpkin pie spice
¼	cup cold water	½	teaspoon salt
1	(16 ounce) can pumpkin	¼	teaspoon vanilla
¾	cup sugar, divided	¾	cup finely chopped walnuts
½	cup milk		
2	large eggs, separated	1	cup whipping cream
		1	9-inch baked pie crust

Soften gelatin in water in 2-quart saucepan. Stir in pumpkin, ½ cup sugar, milk, lightly beaten egg yolks, spice and salt. Heat just to boiling, stirring constantly. Turn heat to low and cook 5 minutes while stirring. Remove from heat, add vanilla and cool. Chill until thickened slightly. Beat egg whites with 2 tablespoons sugar until stiff. Fold into pumpkin mixture with nuts. Whip cream with remaining sugar. Layer half of pumpkin mixture in crust, top with half of whipped cream; top with remaining pumpkin and cream. Refrigerate until ready to serve.

Yield: 6 servings

PEAR CLAFOUTIS

6	Anjou pears	½	cup heavy cream
½	cup pear brandy		Pinch of salt
6	large eggs	1	tablespoon confectioner's sugar
½	cup sugar		
1	teaspoon vanilla		Whipped cream or ice cream
¾	cup plain flour		

Preheat oven to 400°. Peel and core each pear and then cut into thin slices (approximately 16 slices per pear). Place cut pears in a flat bowl or platter and cover with brandy. Stir and let sit for 1 hour. Combine eggs, sugar and vanilla; beat until frothy. Slowly beat in flour, cream and salt. Butter and sugar a 10-inch non-metallic baking dish. Arrange pears in a spiral pattern and add juice. Pour egg batter over pears. Bake for 25 minutes or until top is golden. Cool on a rack; sprinkle with confectioner's sugar. Serve warm or at room temperature, topped with whipped cream or ice cream.

Yield: 8 servings

PARISH HOUSE PECAN PIE

½	cup sugar	3	eggs
½	stick butter	1	cup chopped pecans
1	cup white corn syrup	1	9-inch unbaked pie crust
¼	teaspoon salt		

Preheat oven to 350°. Cream sugar and butter. Add corn syrup and salt. Beat until well blended and mix in eggs, one at a time. Add pecans. Pour into crust and bake for 1 hour or until knife comes out clean.

Yield: 8 servings

CREAMY LEMON FILLING

2	eggs plus 2 egg yolks		Zest of 1 lemon
1	pinch of salt	1	cup sugar
6	tablespoons lemon juice	½	cup butter

Put eggs in double boiler and beat gently. Add rest of ingredients and stir with wooden spoon over gently boiling water until consistency of mayonnaise.

 Use with pound cake and whipped cream.

HOT FUDGE SAUCE

1	(6 ounce) package semi-sweet chocolate chips	1⅓	cups evaporated milk
		1	cup powdered sugar
¼	cup butter	1	teaspoon vanilla

Melt chips and butter. Add milk and sugar, stirring until the mixture comes to a boil. Boil for 5 to 8 minutes, stirring occasionally. Remove from heat; add vanilla. Store in refrigerator until ready to reheat and serve.

 Delicious on ice cream or pound cake.

FRESH STRAWBERRY SAUCE

2 cups fresh strawberries   ¼ teaspoon vanilla
1 tablespoon sugar

Cut berries in halves or quarters. Mix in food processor with sugar for 1 to 2 minutes, leaving strawberries with a few chunks. Add vanilla and stir well. Refrigerate until ready to serve. Sauce will thicken as it cools.

WINE SAUCE

1 cup butter   3 eggs
2 cups sugar   ¼ cup sherry

Mix all ingredients and stir constantly until it comes to a boil.

 Delicious on plum pudding, Boston brown bread or date-nut bread.

APPLESAUCE FRITTERS

½ cup sugar   ¼ teaspoon salt
¼ cup firmly packed brown   ¾ teaspoon cinnamon
      sugar   ½ teaspoon nutmeg
2 eggs   ¼ cup milk
2 tablespoons oil   1 cup applesauce
2¾ cups all-purpose flour   ½ teaspoon vanilla
1½ teaspoons baking powder   Oil for deep frying
½ teaspoon baking soda   Powdered sugar

Combine first 4 ingredients and beat until blended. Combine dry ingredients and add to sugar mixture alternately with milk. Stir in applesauce and vanilla. Heat oil, 2 to 3 inches deep, to 375°. Drop batter by heaping tablespoonfuls into oil, 3 or 4 at a time. Cook 2 minutes on each side until golden. Drain on paper towels and sprinkle with powdered sugar.

Yield: 3 dozen

BANANAS FLAMBÉ

½	cup butter		Vanilla ice cream
½	cup brown sugar	¼	cup rum
6	bananas, sliced lengthwise		

Melt butter in a large pan. Add brown sugar and cook over medium heat until caramelized; stir constantly. Add bananas to the sauce and simmer for 5 minutes. Add rum and light with a match. Let burn until flame goes out. Serve over ice cream.

 Be sure to warm rum before igniting.

Yield: 6 servings

BANANA SHERBET

1	cup sugar	1½	cups orange juice
1	cup water	1	tablespoon lemon juice
2	ripe bananas, mashed		

Mix together sugar and water in a saucepan and heat until sugar dissolves. Combine remaining ingredients and mix well. Gradually add syrup to banana mixture and pour into a shallow pan. Freeze.

 This is a very refreshing summer dessert and is delicious served with pound cake.

Yield: 6 servings

CHOCOLATE LEAVES

1	square of semisweet chocolate	Leaves of your choice from the garden

Melt chocolate and paint on leaves. Put in freezer until chocolate sets. Peel leaf from chocolate and you will have chocolate leaves!

CHERRIES JUBILEE

2	cups pitted black cherries	1	cup Southern Comfort, 86
¾	cup cherry juice		or 100 proof
1	cup white corn syrup		Vanilla ice cream

In a saucepan stir cherries, juice and corn syrup over heat until warm. Add Southern Comfort. Ignite and ladle over individual servings of ice cream.

 This may be done from a chafing dish at the table. A dash of pure lemon extract makes a larger flame.

Yield: 8 servings

CHOCOLATE COVERED STRAWBERRIES

1	(12 ounce) package semi-sweet chocolate bits	½	teaspoon vanilla
6	tablespoons butter		Strawberries with stems

Melt chocolate bits in microwave on high for 2 to 3 minutes. Stir well. When melted, stir in butter and vanilla and cook for another 30 to 40 seconds. Stir and cook until all is melted and smooth. Dip strawberries in chocolate, swirling to coat evenly. Place on wax paper and set in cool, dry place.

 You may roll chocolate-dipped strawberries in finely chopped nuts.

CHOCOLATE CURLS

1	square of semisweet chocolate

Soften chocolate and shave off layer with double-jointed vegetable peeler. Put curls on wax paper in freezer until ready to use.

ICE HOUSE ECLAIRS

Pastry

½	cup water	½	cup flour
¼	cup butter	2	eggs

Filling

¾	cup sugar	2	cups very warm milk
¼	cup flour	3	eggs, beaten

Topping

Melted chocolate   Whipped cream

Preheat oven to 375°. Boil water and butter. Add flour and beat well. Add eggs, one at a time, beating well after each addition. Shape; bake on a cookie sheet for 45 minutes.

For filling, mix sugar and flour in double boiler; add milk. Cook, stirring constantly; add eggs. Remove from heat and cool. When cool, fill shells.

Top with melted chocolate and whipped cream.

Yield: 8 servings

LEMON ICE IN LEMON CUPS

6	large lemons, juiced	1	cup sugar
1	envelope unflavored gelatin	2¼	cups water, divided
			Mint sprigs for garnish

To make cups, remove top half of each lemon. Grate peel and squeeze juice from this portion. Remove pulp from bottom lemon halves; cut a thin slice off the very bottom so the cups will stand up. Refrigerate until serving time. Soak gelatin in ¼ cup water until soft. Cook softened gelatin, sugar and remaining water over low heat until gelatin is thoroughly dissolved. Remove from heat and add lemon zest and juice. Pour mixture into bowl, cover and freeze for 3 hours, until partially frozen. Remove from freezer and beat at medium speed until smooth but still frozen. Re-freeze for 2 hours and repeat process. Freeze until firm. To serve, let ice stand at room temperature for 10 minutes. Scoop into lemon cups and garnish with mint sprigs.

 Lots of steps but very elegant when finished.

Yield: 6 servings

SHERRY ALMANDRADO

Gelatin

1	tablespoon unflavored gelatin	6	egg whites
¼	cup cold water	¼	teaspoon almond extract
¾	cup boiling water	⅓	cup sherry
1	cup sugar	⅓	cup finely chopped almonds

Sauce

2	cups milk	⅛	teaspoon vanilla
6	egg yolks	3	tablespoons sherry
¼	cup sugar	1	cup whipping cream
⅛	teaspoon salt		

Put gelatin in cold water for 5 minutes. Add boiling water and stir until gelatin dissolves. Add sugar and stir. Chill until it begins to thicken. Beat until frothy. Beat egg whites until stiff; add to the beaten gelatin mixture and beat until blended. Add flavoring and sherry. Pour half the mixture into a mold, sprinkle almonds on top and add the other half of the mixture. Cover with waxed paper and chill overnight.

For the sauce, scald milk in double boiler. Beat egg yolks lightly and add sugar and salt. Pour milk slowly into egg mixture. Return to double boiler and cook until mixture coats spoon. Strain. When cool, add vanilla and sherry. Chill overnight. To serve, top gelatin with sherry custard sauce and whipped cream.

Yield: 8 servings

PEACHES AND CREAM SOUP

1½	pounds fresh peaches	¼	teaspoon ground nutmeg
	Water		Pitcher of heavy cream or
½	cup sugar		melted ice cream
1½	tablespoons lemon juice		

Peel, pit and cut peaches into quarters. In a saucepan, cover peaches with water; add sugar, lemon juice and nutmeg. Bring to a boil; simmer until peaches are tender, about 15 minutes. Cool; puree in blender and press through a sieve. Chill thoroughly and serve in small, deep dessert bowls or parfait glasses. Pass a pitcher of heavy cream or melted ice cream.

Yield: 4 servings

FIGS AND RASPBERRIES WITH PORT CREAM

1	cup heavy whipping cream	5-6	tablespoons port wine, no substitute
	Sugar	1	box fresh raspberries
	Vanilla	12	small fresh figs, peeled

Whip cream, adding sugar and vanilla to taste. Add port. Gently mix with raspberries and figs.

Yield: 4 servings

STAINED GLASS WINE JELLY

2	envelopes unflavored gelatin	1	pinch of salt
½	cup cold water	2¼	cups sherry
½	cup boiling water	¼	cup strained lemon juice
⅔	cup sugar	¼	cup strained orange juice
			Whipped cream

In a large bowl, soak gelatin in cold water until softened. Add boiling water and stir until dissolved. Add sugar and salt. Stir until sugar dissolves. Add sherry and juices. Refrigerate until set. With a wooden spoon, chop gelatin into chunks and serve in parfait glasses or deep dessert dishes. Top with whipped cream or custard sauce.

 Especially good and refreshing after a big Christmas dinner!

Yield: 6 servings

INDEX

CONTRIBUTORS

The Episcopal Church Women of St. Paul's express their gratitude to the members and friends who shared their recipes and contributed their talents for *Take The Tour*. We claim no originality for the recipes; we can only attest to their excellence. Due to availability of space, the cookbook committee regrets that it was impossible to include all of the wonderful recipes submitted.

Emily Greer Amburn
Janet Hebel Armstrong
Louise Cranford Artman
Judy Baker
Lisa Hoenig Baker
Kaye Hollowell Barker
Grace Adams Bean
Harvey Livingston Binns
Pam Ingram Blizard
Page Bolz
Alice Weadon Bond
Snooky Phipps Bond
Rheta Bonner
Debra Ellis Boyle
Bettie Bonner Bradshaw
Kathryn Brown
Anne Errickson Bruce
Joe Brucia
Harriet Bryan
Maxine and Norm Bullard
Carolyn Smith Burns
Christine Carter
Carolyn Cassell
Judy and John Chilcoat
Sharie Clark
Barbara Mobley Conger
Nellie Rose Conger
Kim Elmore Cooper
Pat Coyne
Marcia Kepler Crandall
Monika Maitre Creighton
Susan Binns Creighton
Margaret Smith Davis
Jean Hicks DeMajewski
Mary Burns Detgen
Norma Dirom
Betty Bobbitt Dixon
Susan Dotterer Dixon
Jane Franklin Edwards
Hazel Shaw Elliott
Mary Devereaux Elliott
Anne Detgen Ellis
Kathleen Happel Elmore
Cindy Fields
Darcy Gaines
Martha Edwards Garst
Mary Woodward Germann

Anna Bristol Giles
Ronda and Jack Goff
Dorothy Graham
Lena Habit Griffin
Martha Guttu
Virginia Harbert
Clara Capehart Harney
Missie and Scotty Harrell
Susan Boolay Harvey
Betsy Shepard Hassell
Frances Elaine Held
Sandy Stalter Hendee
Lois Bush Herbert
Georgia Holmes Hines
Helen Yentz Hoffman
Virginia Harris Holland
Rachel Holmes
Lindsay Britt Hornthal
Sadie Hobbs Hoskins
Frances Drane Inglis
Jeanie Inglis
Burton Hathaway Jones
Mary Lou Jones
Nellie Rawls Jones
Sherry Nance Jordan
Janet Fuller Kay
Linda Edwards Keel
Opal Wright Kehayes
Cordelia Kelly
Susan Anne Knighton
Penny McCurry Krell
Linda Varin Lane
Martha Conger Leary
Ginny Long
Lina Pruden Mack
Marian Martin
Joan Carawan Maxwell
Peggy Barker Miller
Ann and Charles Morgan
Margaret Mullen
Edith Bond Nixon
Nada Ann Noble
Shirley Cross Parker
Anne Shepard Parrish
Marie White Perry
Warner Burch Perry
Ruth Burnette Phillips

Pat Storie Polk
Emma Cherry Powell
Susan and John Powell
Nancy Walker Pruden
Carolyn White Raines
Jane Riddick
Gloria Rivers
Nancy Gifford Roberson
Georgina Ferguson Robison
Gertrude Shepard Rosevear
Wanda Rossman
Reidun Einersen Shapter
Rebecca Walker Shepard
Carol Ellison Sieck
Leona Woodring Smith
Victoria Varner Smith
Betty Jo Spencer
Georgena Drake Stalter
Carolyn Summerville
Mary Anne Thomas
Laura Lee Ticknor
Elizabeth Townsend
Kathleen Bell Townsend
Mary Bradham Tucker
Nancy Bissell Turpin
Sally Reed Underhill
Anne Elizabeth Vaughan
Peggy Anne and Roland
　Vaughan
Peggy Walklet
Debbie Welker
Elizabeth Will
Kit Forehand Williams
Margaret Williams
Beth Bissett Willis
Edna Harvey Wolverton
Annette Fairless Wood
Leila Budlong Wood
Mary Gregg Wood
Nancy Trask Wood
Nell Riddick Wood
Susan Hemingway Wood
Virginia Hall Wood
Harriett Mardre Woolard
Angie Woodruff Wright
Margaret Sanders Wright
Rebecca Wright

Take The Tour
St. Paul's Episcopal Church Women
P. O. Box 548
Edenton, NC 27932-0548
(252) 482-3522

Please send ____ copies of *Take The Tour* @ $17.95 each _____
Postage and handling @ $ 3.00 each _____
North Carolina residents add sales tax @ $ 1.08 each _____
TOTAL _____

Name _____

Address _____

City _____ State ____ Zip _____

Make checks payable to *St. Paul's ECW*

- -

Take The Tour
St. Paul's Episcopal Church Women
P. O. Box 548
Edenton, NC 27932-0548
(252) 482-3522

Please send ____ copies of *Take The Tour* @ $17.95 each _____
Postage and handling @ $ 3.00 each _____
North Carolina residents add sales tax @ $ 1.08 each _____
TOTAL _____

Name _____

Address _____

City _____ State ____ Zip _____

Make checks payable to *St. Paul's ECW*

- -

Take The Tour
St. Paul's Episcopal Church Women
P. O. Box 548
Edenton, NC 27932-0548
(252) 482-3522

Please send ____ copies of *Take The Tour* @ $17.95 each _____
Postage and handling @ $ 3.00 each _____
North Carolina residents add sales tax @ $ 1.08 each _____
TOTAL _____

Name _____

Address _____

City _____ State ____ Zip _____

Make checks payable to *St. Paul's ECW*